Waugh

Auberon Waugh is the e[...]
and a regular contribu[...]
numerous other publications, [...]
Queen and *Tatler*.

Waugh on Wine

AUBERON WAUGH

Edited by Jan Fry

Illustrations by
William Rushton

Fontana/Collins

First published in Great Britain by
Fourth Estate Ltd 1986
This edition first published
in 1987 by Fontana Paperbacks
8 Grafton Street, London W1X 3LA

Copyright © Auberon Waugh 1986

Illustrations by William Rushton

Made and printed in Great Britain by
William Collins Sons & Co. Ltd, Glasgow

CONTENTS

THE REST OF THE WORLD

PEOPLE AND PLACES

ACKNOWLEDGEMENTS

The author and publisher would like to
acknowledge the following companies for their
permission to use some of the material included in
this book:

Berry Bros & Rudd Ltd
Number Three Saint James's Street

Conde Nast
Tatler

Christie's Wine Publications Ltd
Christie's Wine Book

National Magazines Ltd
Harper's & Queen

Robert Adkinson Ltd
The Académie du Vin Wine Cellar Book

Spectator Ltd
Spectator

INTRODUCTION

I first became a wine-writer at the request of an old friend, Tina Brown, who had recently been made editor of *Tatler*, the 'society' magazine. Remembering Bertram Wooster, whose one contribution to English letters was an article on 'What the Well-Dressed Young Man is Wearing' in a similar publication, I assumed that as a life-long wine-drinker I knew all that anyone really needed to know about the subject. Those who knew more, and could talk about such things as grape varieties, were prigs and pedants. In fact, in a lifetime of scribbling about every subject under the sun, I had even written about wine once or twice, although none of these earlier writings is included in this collection. In fact I rather blush to think of them now. In one of them, as I remember, I advised *Spectator* readers to have nothing to do with the 1975 vintage in Bordeaux, as being disgracefully overpriced, in order to teach the greedy Bordelais a lesson. Nobody who followed that advice will have thanked me after watching price rises since the great 1982 vintage, although it is true that many 1975s seem to be taking a long time to show the quality which experts still assure us is there. In another article, written at a moment of political despondency, I unquestioningly accepted the unscrupulous advice of an acquaintance in the wine trade that 1975 would prove the greatest port vintage since 1963 and advised readers to invest all their savings in it. Equities were a minefield, I said, since nobody could expect the British worker to work; money invested in gilts or fixed-interest securities might just as well be given to the socialist government, at the existing rates of inflation; works of art were liable to theft or seizure. The only thing to do with money was to put it in 1975 ports.

Never can worse advice have been given. The year turned out to produce thin, forward wines which have scarcely increased in value and are not expected to improve. Although they are perfectly pleasant to drink now (1986 and 1987) so long as they are not compared to any other vintage, I would hate to think that there are families with crates and crates of this uninspiring beverage who had hoped that it had secured their old age.

In fact it was only after becoming *Tatler*'s wine correspondent that I began to appreciate my own ignorance of the subject – or what a vast and fascinating subject it was. Despite my bravado in accepting the post – it was not at all well paid, but I hoped to benefit by a certain increased stature in the eyes of wine merchants – I judged it prudent to write under a pseudonym, and chose the quaint pen-name of Crispin de St Crispian. Crispin had aleady decided on two main planks of his campaign to make the world a better place for wine-drinkers. In the first place, hosts who skimp on their wine should be exposed, ridiculed and humiliated. In the second place wine-writing should be approached from a position which is always several degrees over the top.

Crispin de St Crispian continued to write his somewhat hyperbolical column on the wine scene until Tina went off to edit *Vanity Fair* in New York and I took the column, in slightly more sober dress and written under my own name, to *Harper's and Queen*.

While Crispin was in full flow, the *Spectator* – a magazine to which I have been contributing a weekly political, literary or current affairs column, with few interruptions, for nearly twenty years – decided that it wanted to start its own Wine Club. I was given the task of organising it, choosing the wines and writing the descriptions of them which would help *Spectator* readers decide whether or not they wished to buy. It was my first experience of writing what amounted to advertising copy, although, having chosen the wines, I could defend myself by pointing out that my enthusiasms, for what they were worth, were genuine.

My first experience as a wine-writer, on the *Tatler*, convinced me that of all journalistic specialities, wine-writing was the least influential. Generally speaking, if I praised a wine, nobody bought it, if I criticised a wine – and, gracious, how rude I was – nobody shunned it. Wine merchants were happy to be mentioned, but it made no measurable difference to their sales. This might have been galling for someone who had spent many years as a book reviewer in newspapers where a few words of praise immediately sold several hundred copies, and where a rave review might even sell a thousand. In fact, I was rather relieved, since the effect of making a wine more popular is almost invariably to increase its price.

In fact only one wine merchant reported a significant demand for a particular wine after I had praised it in *Tatler*. The wine, as I remember, cost under £2 a bottle, and the wine merchant was sold out within hours. The bitter lesson of this was that even *Tatler* readers – supposedly among the richest and freest-spending in the land – were obsessed by the horrid English desire to buy only the cheapest wine.

Fortunately, *Spectator* readers are a different breed. What they really like are grand old Burgundies and mature, classified clarets – almost impossible to find except in very small quantities and at exorbitant prices. Since my own tastes are exactly the same, I spend a large part of my time hunting down parcels of old wine which are going cheap, either because they come from a vintage which has been officially declared poor by the various charts which people find in their diaries (one can find some wonderful wines even in such unlikely years as 1972 and 1977 in Bordeaux, 1974 and 1980 in Burgundy) or because a wine merchant decides he needs cash in a hurry.

But the joys of writing about wine – and also of reading about it – are quite different. I find some of my happiest hours nowadays, between editing the *Literary Review* and writing newspaper columns, are spent reading wine lists. My terror is that as Britons work less and less hard, less and less efficiently, this in time will become the only thing we can do. The days when we actually drank the stuff will be no more than a happy memory. Much of the material in these pages deals with the problem of finding substitutes for the classic wines of Bordeaux and Burgundy which we can no longer afford. In time, perhaps, we will not even be able to afford Barolo from Italy, Chilean Cabernet, South African pinotage, Australian Chardonnay or those little-known French country wines which people still keep discovering. In that case, we will be left with our memories, to which these pages may make some contribution. The only piece of advice I feel able to pass on, the only certain wisdom I have acquired in the best part of half a century, is that anyone with money to spend should spend it on laying down a cellar.

Auberon Waugh
July 1986

WAUGH AT LARGE

Perils of Being a Wine-writer

I have a cousin who lives near me. He is much richer than I am, with an acreage of fat fields in Somerset and Devon which puts him well into the millionaire class. For some reason, although he is a generous host in other ways, he always serves filthy wine – the cheapest jug reds from Spain which he buys in ten-gallon plastic containers. On one occasion he produced a drink of such stupendous horror that I was inspired to write a column in the *Tatler* – then edited by Tina Brown – denouncing the English upper-class habit of serving cheap wine at meals. They would never dream of serving inferior cuts of beef, or scrag-end of lamb. Why did they think they could get away with nasty wine?

The trouble was that although there is a well-worn vocabulary of praise to describe good wine – it can be muscular, well-knit, complex, fragrant, etc. – there is no equivalent glossary to describe what is bad. The foul beverage itself tasted of vinegar, blue ink and curry powder, but such a bald description gave no hint of the shock, or disappointment, even the sadness of such a discovery. After playing with the idea of comparing it to a collapsed marquee fallen into a rotting silage pit, I eventually decided that it reminded me of a bunch of dead chrysanthemums on the grave of a stillborn West Indian baby. It was in that form that my cousin's wine was used as an object lesson for the readers of *Tatler*.

Shortly after my article appeared, Tina Brown received a letter from the Press Council saying it had received a complaint from a midwife in the London borough of Camden, which complaint was being backed by her local representative on the Race Relations Board. In due course, we were summoned to appear before the Council in full session – Tina in a ravishingly elegant grey knitwear two-piece, I in a dark blue suit and white collar.

Was I suggesting that the wine was nastier by virtue of reminding me of a West Indian baby? Not at all, I said. The metaphor of a dead piccaninny was used for the greater poignancy of the image it evoked. The West Indian connection was also explained by reference to curried mangoes which, although admirable things in themselves, were out of place among the tastes in a bottle of wine. After due deliberation, the Press Council acquitted us both of any intention to excite racial hatred, or to affront the sensitivities of any ethnic group. So we walked free. It was the first time any editor of the *Tatler* had appeared before that august body. I suspect it will be the last time any wine correspondent is summoned to explain and justify his comments on a particular bottle of wine.

The results of this episode were two-fold. First, and most important, my cousin started taking slightly more trouble over the wine he served. Second, another brave publishing initiative bit the dust:

> One task more declined, one more footpath untrod,
> One more triumph for devils and sorrow for angels,
> One wrong more to man, one more insult to God!
> *Robert Browning*

In other words, Tina has learned her lesson, and wine-writing has resumed its former course. No more collapsed marquees or poignant grave-markers. Looking at a recent edition of *Vanity Fair,* where she now reigns, I found an interesting and informative article on the Pinot Noir varietal wines of California and Oregon, by Joel L. Fleishman. I was particularly interested in this article because I have been searching for some time for a good Pinot Noir from anywhere except Burgundy, so far with very little success. My cellar has perhaps 500 or 600 red Burgundies quietly maturing, but it occurred to me after completing my purchase of the 1983 vintage that red Burgundy prices have become so high in the better communes and domaines that I will probably never buy any more. Hence the desperate search for a substitute. Mr Fleishman tasted twenty-one American Pinot Noirs, and picked out seven of them as especially worthwhile. Of these seven, five were described in the following terms:

(a) 'A bouquet of tobacco infused with a beautiful perfume and a flavor of ripe cherries . . .'
(b) '. . . powerful dark-cherry fruit, slightly smoky in taste . . .'
(c) 'a bouquet of ripe berries, with hints of rose petals and lavender, and intense, complex, fruit flavors'
(d) 'an intense flavor of cherries, dry, not sweet, with a "chewiness" not detected in any of the other wines'
(e) 'A closed-in bouquet but lush, well-knit, and well-balanced smoky cherry flavors'

The overwhelming impression seems to be of cherries and smoke. I am not criticising Mr Fleishman's taste or vocabulary. Plainly cherries and smoke are the things to look for in American Pinot Noir. When describing tastes, one is bound to use some sort of shorthand, in any case, unless one is to embark on some baroque poetic fantasy on every occasion. It reads oddly to me only because neither cherries nor smoke have yet reached Europe as a way of describing wine. I have been eating cherries all my life, and breathing in smoke for much of it, but I have never found a Burgundy which tasted of either – let alone of tobacco, perfume, rose petals or lavender. If I found one of my wines tasting of any of those things I would send it back and demand an explanation. It is true that I once thought I detected a hint of cigar smoke in a Joseph Phelps Chardonnay I was given at a British Academy of Gastronomes lunch. But I had been told to look for it, and decided eventually that the smell probably came from my neighbour, a nice fat *Sunday Times* journalist called Godfrey Smith, who was smoking a cigar.

But we wine buffs talk of Burgundy as being 'velvety' or 'silken' and use an entire alternative glossary which is every bit as misleading or meaningless. In fact, the number of words which can usefully be used to describe or assess wine is limited. Apart from the obvious words of appreciation or dismissal – good, bad; sweet, sour; too little taste or too much – it can be fined down to about six technical considerations. These are the strength and balance of alcohol, acid, tannin, fruit, sugar, the degree of concentration and state of maturity. We all know – the wine buffs, that is – what sort of taste should be produced by each grape varietal or blend, and this is assessed in discussion of the 'fruit'. But not everybody who drinks wine is a wine buff, and wine articles would be unreadable if writers confined themselves to these technical measurements. Hence the clusters of cherries, the bottles of perfume and wads of tobacco, the baskets-full of strawberry, raspberry, gooseberry, pomegranate, passion fruit and mango called in to help the poor wine-writers describe a taste. I am not sure how helpful any of them are. It is one thing to be discussing a wine with various friends who are drinking it too – some of the most enjoyable conversations I have ever had have been on that basis – but quite another when you are trying to describe the taste of a particular wine to someone who probably is reading your piece immediately after breakfast or under the hair dryer.

My own feeling, despite several unhappy experiences, is that wine-writing should be camped up: the writer should never like a wine, he should be in love with it; never find a wine disappointing but identify it as a mortal enemy, an attempt to poison him; sulphuric acid should be discovered where there is the faintest hint of sharpness. Bizarre and improbable side-tastes should be proclaimed: mushrooms, rotting wood, black treacle, burned pencils, condensed milk, sewage, the smell of French railway stations or ladies' underwear – anything to get away from the accepted list of fruit and flowers. As I say, I am not sure that it helps much, but it is more amusing to read.

Until fairly recently, it was considered rude in polite upper-class society to make any comment at all on food or wine. To praise it was as boorish as to hint at criticism. Anything offered was assumed to be of the best. It was even ruder to notice a hostess's furniture or pictures. This is changing now, as servants disappear and the hostess herself is usually responsible for cooking, but old-fashioned and grand people, living in the country, still tend to look a bit startled when guests start praising their food, wine or appointments. This polite convention may explain why the food and wine in many country houses were so foul, why all the carpets were bald, the chintzes covered in dogs' hairs. But one of the perils of being a wine-writer is that guests always expect to be given something memorable in the way of wine when they come to your home.

The trouble with this expectation is that the best wines are now prodigiously expensive. Where even fifteen years ago any reasonably well-off person could reckon to fill his cellar with premiers crus Bordeaux, and grands crus Burgundies, now only the very rich indeed can even think of drinking such wines – starting, as they do, at about £30–£35 the bottle for a wine which will not be ready to drink for another fifteen years.

My own solution is to search for unusual wines which provide guests with something to talk about – even a sense of discovery – without ruining the host. Very few people realise how cripplingly expensive the best wine is nowadays. They will think it quite normal to be served a Château Haut-Brion, and reckon themselves short-changed if they are given a Beychevelle or a Léoville–Las Cases. Instead, I search the world to find examples of pre-phylloxera Cabernet from Chile, rare and honeyed Chardonnays from Australia or Gewürztraminers from New Zealand, Chenins Blancs from South Africa, even Zinfandels from California. Perhaps my most successful discovery has been a Cabernet from the Lebanon called Château Musar, made by a genius called Serge Hochar who trained in Bordeaux at Château Léoville–Barton. This is a really superb wine ... as soon as the Americans discover it, its price will go through the roof.

Then I will have to go on my travels again – to Provence, where they are beginning to make some seriously good, thick red wine from such Bordeaux grapes as Cabernet Sauvignon, Merlot and Malbec, as well as importing Syrah from the northern Rhône and Cinsault from the South. Or Bulgaria, whose heavily subsidised Cabernets are beginning to be discovered, unfortunately, at the cheap end of the market. There are many good minor wines from the Loire, too, while Spain and northern Italy are both making huge strides in the quality of their production.

An Englishman's Cellar

My house in Somerset has nine cellars, stretching underneath the greater part of the house. In former times they provided sleeping and living accommodation for the lower servants as well as one wine cellar and a village lock-up, which is picturesquely called the dungeon and might prove too damp for storing wine. It has mysterious hooks hanging from the ceiling which, we tell ourselves, were probably used for curing hams. That will be the last cellar to be fitted with racks, but my life's ambition is to fill all nine by the time my youngest child leaves university and starts earning his own living. Then I will settle down to an early retirement at about fifty-one and drink my way through all nine cellars in the years that remain to me.

The reasoning behind this Doomsday approach is partly political, partly economic. I do not think the British will be able to buy good French wine for much longer. In any case, I do not trust the government to protect savings, and do not trust the British worker enough to invest in equities. The only certain requirements in life are warmth, good food and good wine. I have a thirty-five-acre smallholding to provide the food and fuel; the best investment for old age must be wine. After the age of fifty-one, I plan to retire from journalism in a benign alcoholic haze and write drivelling novels which few people will want to read.

So far I have filled three cellars, but with all the wine of the 1983 vintage which I have bought, and which is still lying in cellars all over Europe or on its way to Somerset, I will have filled five. Perhaps I should deal with the 1983 purchases first, since they are the most recent. I have bought no 1983 claret, having over-extended myself – for a Burgundian – on the 1982 vintage. In fact the only 1983 Bordeaux I have bought is from Sauternes – a case of

An Englishman's Cellar

Climens and two of Rieussec. As I believe in drinking Sauternes younger than most Englishmen – I find I actually enjoy the 1976s more than the 1967s – I will probably start drinking in six years' time. The general agreement seems to be that the 1983 clarets, while very good, are overshadowed by the 1982s, and since they are no cheaper there seemed no point in buying the 1983s. Although I have attended numerous tastings of both years en primeur I find I have neither the aptitude nor the inclination to judge clarets en primeur and take other people's word for it. My 1982 purchases were five cases of Léoville–Las Cases, at a time when they were still going for £145 the case ex-cellars, and three cases of Pichon Baron, which I believe may prove to be one of the greatest bargains of the whole 1982 vintage at £65 the case ex-cellars.

Where Burgundy was concerned, I decided to make my first major purchases since the 1978 vintage. They all taste utterly disgusting to me, but I know and trust John Avery, of Avery's in Bristol, whom I believe to be the best judge of Burgundy in Britain, and ordered thirteen cases of his 1983 Burgundy offer from his own tasting notes, going like an arrow for anything he described as 'almost sweet', 'old style', 'concentrated' and 'dark'. In the course of innumerable tastings, I have picked up various other cases here and there, but by and large I have found too much paleness, too much of light weight, much too much tannin and a terrifying lack of sweetness. I did not buy any 1982 Burgundy except a light one from Peter Dominic for immediate drinking and an exceptionally good medium-weight Burgundy from the Auxerrois at somewhere called Coulanges la Vineuse which Morgan Furze discovered.

From the brilliant white Burgundies of 1983, I chose a Meursault from someone called Dupont-Fahn which Harvey's of Bristol produced at a Cockburn tasting in London, and a spectacular Mâcon-Viré from André Bonhomme which David Stevens, of Oxford, discovered.

I have no German, Alsatian or Loire wines in my cellar – not because I do not buy them occasionally but because, like Californian wines, I do not feel they are cellar material. Where Germany is concerned, the 1976s are still so cheap from Hallgarten that I am reluctant to waste cellar space on the 1983s, excellent as they undoubtedly are.

Where the 1983 ports are concerned, I am still dithering about which to buy. Taylor strikes me as the best, but I am not sure I will be around long enough to drink it. I might settle for a mixture of Taylor and Graham. The first of my three cellars is taken up entirely with port, apart from some clarets which I have never unpacked from their wooden cases, so remote do they seem from drinking. This cellar is barrel-vaulted with brick bins. One bin is devoted to 1963 ports (mostly Fonseca, some Martinez I bought for a song in Taunton, a few Warre and some oddments); the next is given to more oddments: some 1965 Taylor's Vargellas (absolutely delicious and still able to be bought quite reasonably from Berry Bros), the rest of my 1966s – mostly Croft's – and a dozen of Cockburn's 1967 which I fancied at a tasting. My 1970s bin seems almost entirely taken up with Quinta do Noval – I do not know why. Somebody must have recommended it to me. The best buy in vintage ports nowadays, I would say, is the 1975 vintage. Although the trade sneers at them, and they do not stand up well when tasted with other years, the truth is that one does not drink one's port with other vintages and if drunk alone they will soon make a very satisfactory port taste in the mouth – at half the price of a 1966 and less than a quarter the price of a 1963. My 1975 bin is embarrassingly full – mostly Warre but some Cockburn, some Graham and one or two others. The 1977s take two bins – Taylor, Fonseca and Warre – but I do not suppose I will be tasting them for another twelve years, possibly fifteen or sixteen, by which time I will be sixty, and possibly forbidden to drink port. I still can't make up my mind about the 1983s.

The next cellar is much bigger, with fitted racks up two of the walls to head level and an old apple-rack for magnums in the middle. I divide it into vertical sections, each section of six holes horizontally, sixteen holes vertically. This cellar is called, rather unEnglishly, the cave de garde (as opposed to the port cellar, which is called cave de vieillissement). Since most of the individual wines in this cellar have disappeared from the market, I shall not gloat over many individual bottles, but might mention some of the dud ones which will eventually be moved to the dungeon when I have equipped it as a 'sin bin' for all the mistakes I have made. A better-organised man would probably sell them, but it seems rather mean to pass them on.

The first section is all 1972 Burgundies. It used to be 1969s but they have been moved to the next cellar – for current drinking – and are disappearing fast. Best in the 1972 section is Remoissenet's Musigny from Avery's. Most of a five-case order for Louis Jadot's 1972 Bonne Mares which I bought in a rush of blood to the head from young Nick Davies in Hungerford – a good wine but sharper than it should be – and there is some dud Chambolle-Musigny 1972 from Bouchard which is still fizzing after thirteen years.

Next section is 1976 Burgundies, some lovely wines spoiled by twenty-three bottles of a Morey St Denis from Harvey's which has turned undrinkably (and I should guess irredeemably) sour. There is also a 1976 Santenay Gravières from Avery which was wandering when last tasted, but might yet pull itself together. Next section is entirely devoted to 1976 déclassé Burgundies from Avery – marvellous wines, sold for a song, but unobtainable now. The best are called Cuvée Suzanne Le Goux, which tastes amazingly like a Vosne-Romanée Les Suchots and Cuvée du Dragon, almost indistinguishable from Nuits St-Georges Les St-Georges. Last section on this wall is devoted to the Northern Rhône – mostly 1978s (Jaboulet's Hermitage La Chapelle, which everyone says will be terrific in thirteen years' time and a number of Côtes Roties – notably Delas – but also some 1982s – La Chapelle). The Rhônes will be enormously expanded when my 1983 orders come in – Hermitage, Cornas, etc. – and might even merit a cellar to themselves. Perhaps I will brick it up for fifteen years and try to forget about it.

The next wall starts with miscellaneous clarets of no great interest. Next comes a curious section devoted entirely to Château Musar from the Lebanon – 1977s and 1978s, eight dozen of them. I happen to adore this wine, and know, from drinking old vintages, that it turns into something pretty miraculous. It is still amazingly cheap, and the 1977s, by my reckoning, are already showing every characteristic of a great wine.

The next section is devoted to miscellaneous white wines, including a conspicuously dud 1978 Chassagne Montrachet from Chanson and some very dull 1975 Château Broustet, Sauternes. Finally there is a section of Southern Rhônes, mostly Châteauneuf of 1978 and 1979. This will eventually be joined by four cases of Jaboulet's Gigondas 1983 which I bought having tasted a 1967 of this wine in the Escargot Restaurant, Greek Street. I never knew that Gigondas could rise to such heights. But that is another one for bricking up, I fear.

My final cellar has everything for current drinking. I must not gloat about the highlights, but perhaps I might list a few: a selection of 1969 Burgundies from Avery (Nuits St-Georges Les Roncières, Chambolle Musigny); Berry Bros' marvellous 1961 Beaune Clos du Roy from Doudet Naudin; a glorious Château Le Gay, Pomerol, 1966, also from Berry Bros; Brown Bros' Chardonnay 1980 (Australia); CVNE's Viña Real 1970 from Laymont and Shaw; Jaboulet's 1967 Châteauneuf Les Cèdres from Loeb; English-bottled 1971 Charmes Chambertin from Berry Bros; 1967 and 1976 Rieussec, Guiraud, etc., etc. This cellar also has its duds, destined for the sin bin: a shocking 1973 Château Talbot; some rotten 1975 Châteauneuf-du-Papes; some 1978 Fronsacs I bought when there was a craze for them. In this cellar is kept all my champagne (Billecart Salmon and a lovely wine called De Telmont N.V. from Majestic Warehouses) and all ordinary wines which are in only occasional demand: Chilean pre-phylloxera Cabernets; Retsinas; Zinfandels which I like but nobody else does.

The main trouble with my cellars is that they are haunted by bats. By law, nowadays, you are not allowed to kill, frighten or even disturb bats. That is the caring society's revenge on me for my pleasures. But bats are a fairly small price to pay.

Wines to Impress

The great justification for wine snobbery is that it enhances the pleasure of drinking good wine. Knowing a wine's history, that it comes from a particularly prized vineyard or château in a year which is universally acknowledged to be one of the best, makes one pause over one's glass and take it more seriously, reflecting, perhaps, on one's good fortune to be drinking it when so many other people want to be drinking it, too.

Against this, the great crime of wine snobbery is that it has made nonsense of the economics of wine-drinking. The very best is now so grotesquely over-priced in relation to the best that very few Britons who wish to cut a dash or impress their guests can begin to afford it. There are other ways of impressing guests with one's wine, of course. You can produce some minor, unclassified claret with a name which nobody knows and swear that you discovered it on some dusty roadside in Bordeaux, that it has the subtlety of a Lafite, the complexity of a Latour, the fruitiness of a Mouton-Rothschild, the spicy depth of a Château Margaux, the gravelled austerity of an Haut-Brion. The trouble with this method of impressing people is that it very seldom works. However much effort you put into the spiel, your guests will decide you are a mean old pseud.

The trouble is that any other way of impressing people with wine is vilely expensive. American millionaires who wish to impress their guests – and the same is true of American actors and actresses, confidence tricksters, business contacts, would-be swindlers and almost everyone else in that acutely image-conscious nation – demand to have the very best. Unfortunately for British wine-drinkers, the very best is easy to identify. Where claret is concerned, it is the four premiers crus of the Médoc and one of Graves listed above – Château Lafite, Latour, Margaux, Mouton-Rothschild and Haut-Brion – with one premier grand cru from St Emilion, Château Cheval Blanc, and one from Pomerol, Château Petrus. In Sauternes there is Château d'Yquem. In Burgundy, there is anything which bears the magic name of Romanée Conti on the label. When they drink champagne, they insist on Dom Perignon. That is all the Americans know and all they need to know. They can afford the soaring prices which result in these particular wines, so that Château d'Yquem, for instance, is usually between five and eight times the price of its nearest runners-up – Châteaux Guiraud, Coutet, Climens, Suduiraut and Rieussec. Britons simply cannot afford these prices, except for a tiny handful. Unless one is well known to be the Duke of Westminster, or Lord Cowdray or Lord Vestey, it is a waste of time pretending to be any of them. Nobody will be much impressed and some will be downright suspicious to be served a bottle of wine costing more than £100. It is also a wicked waste of money, when there is so much truly excellent wine to be found at a tenth of that price, and a few like Château Musar from the Lebanon or Viña Real 1970 from Rioja or Brown Bros' Chardonnay from Milawa, N.E. Victoria, at little more than a twentieth of these prices.

But my purpose is not to point out wines which are of exceptionally good value. It is to advise on how to impress people. Oddly enough, vast quantities of the premiers crus and premiers grands crus listed above are still bought in Britain. The 1982 vintage, which was a very plentiful one in Bordeaux, reduced the whole market to absurdity when French growers decided to limit the stocks they were prepared to release. Their purpose in doing this was only partly to push prices up. They also wanted to avoid the new socialist taxes and have something for a thin year. But the result was that the premiers crus listed above started selling for anything up to £40 a bottle ex-cellars Bordeaux. This means that you are paying £40 for a bottle which you will not be able to drink for twenty or twenty-five years or even see for two years, when you will have to pay a further £7.60–£8.20 per bottle in carriage, Excise Duty and VAT.

Yet the amazing thing is that these wines were being snapped up on the London market as soon as they appeared. Château Petrus was the most expensive of all, as a result of the American passion for Pomerol, closely followed by Lafite which present fashion places (I think wrongly) a neck ahead of Latour. The 'bargain' of the group was Cheval Blanc, from St Emilion, which at one time was selling for as little as £22.90 a bottle ex-cellars. This one might even be drinking in fifteen years' time.

Presumably, these wines are being bought as an investment, rather than with the vague plan of impressing a guest in twenty-five years' time. Even so, it does not seem to make sense. A total investment of £36.40 on a single bottle of Château Margaux 1982 would represent, at a compound interest rate of 5 per cent, an investment of £123.25 in twenty-five years' time. This makes no allowance whatever for inflation. Whereas in point of fact a bottle of Château Margaux 1959 – there is no reason to be certain that the 1982 will be any better than this magnificent vintage – can be bought from Reid Wines for around £80.27, and this price includes twenty-five years of the worst inflation ever experienced in Britain.

I could bore on for pages to illustrate my thesis that investment in wine is a mug's game. On top of the fact that wine laid down scarcely keeps up with inflation on the purchase price let alone showing a profit, there is the considerable mark-up between selling and buying, with further doses of VAT. And on top of this, I am almost sure that the premier cru Bordeaux bubble is going to burst in the course of the next five or ten years as American buyers become more interested in their own excellent Cabernet Sauvignon from California's Napa Valley. When I was last in New York a Robert Mondavi Cabernet Sauvignon Reserve of 1979 cost £80 – a beautiful wine, but an absurd price. It has huge concentration, like all the best Californian wines, but none of the complexity of the best Bordeaux. On the other hand, few American millionaires are interested in these finer points, and they generally share a sharper interest in value for money than Europeans credit. The only thing which keeps Bordeaux fashionable in America, I feel, is the present strength of the American dollar against European currencies – and that is something which will probably disappear after President Reagan, if not before then.

These are my reasons for arguing that where wines-to-impress are concerned there is nothing to be gained by looking to the future. Those determined to cut a dash with their wines would do best to buy mature wines now. These can be found at regular wine auctions held by Christie's and Sotheby's – irregularly by some provincial auctioneers – or at a diminishing number of wine merchants, such as Berry Bros or Corney and Barrow, who still offer fine wines of considerable age. Christopher Collins, of Bibendum, has enormous stocks of these prodigiously expensive clarets, but I suspect him of catering for investors as much as for drinkers. The only shop I have found which offers an enormous variety of old and unusual wines – often it has only a couple of bottles of each, and resembles a wine museum as much as a shop – is Reid Wines of Hallatrow, near Bristol.

Champagne is essential before any meal which is intended to impress. Any substitute is a complete waste of time, since it will neither impress nor, in most cases, taste very nice. As with claret, magnums are a good idea as they cost no more, look more festive, and one never drinks fewer than two bottles. Krug is undoubtedly the most impressive name in champagne, followed by Pol Roger, Pommery, Veuve Clicquot and the rest of the grandes marques almost indistinguishably. Although the British drink more champagne per head than any other country except France, my impression is that they do not like it much. This is because we generally serve *brut*, the driest of all champagne. If you want your guests to enjoy themselves as well as being impressed, serve an extra sec or a vintage brut which is blander and less sharp.

As a white wine with the first course, I would avoid the famous white Burgundies – Meursault, Grand Cru Chablis, Corton-Charlemagne, Le Montrachet and the rest – because although they are absolutely delicious they are also extremely expensive and few people except wine freaks know about them, or how much they cost. In other words, their price-impression factor is low. If you really want to impress a wine-lover, serve a Condrieu from the Rhône – cheapest from Les Amis du Vin. The only other merchants which have this exquisite wine, so far as I know, are Yapp Bros and O. W. Loeb. Otherwise serve a Hugel's Gewürztraminer or Pinot Blanc d'Alsace, both of which are fresh and lively and seem to show some knowledge of the subject. For a red wine I would choose one of the minor châteaux of St Emilion in a known year –

1978, 1976, 1975, 1971, 1970, 1966. Everybody likes them, nobody really knows his minor châteaux of St Emilion, and they cost about half what a classified château of similar quality from the Médoc will cost.

Any Sauternes will create quite an impression with the pudding – the IEC Wine Society has an absolutely magnificent one called Château Filhot – but last year there was a craze for Muscat de Beaumes de Venise, an extravagantly powerful sweet drink which tastes of dessert grapes. I have a feeling that next year's craze will be for pink champagne. It is not particularly sweet, but goes very well with most puddings and certainly adds a touch of class. The grandest is the Krug Rosé brut, available from Fortnum's. It is closely followed by Pommery's Rosé and the Laurent-Perrier Rosé at about the same price. But where pink champagne is concerned, some of the minor houses produce an excellent wine which is much cheaper: J. Lasalle from Bibendum and Bruno Paillard Rosé from Wineheads stand out. For more impressionable guests, especially young ladies, pink champagne is all that is required to achieve the necessary effect.

From Pint to Glass

A thunderclap of sorts was heard in the wine trade in November 1985 with the publication of a report by Stowell's of Chelsea which pointed out the extent to which table wine has overtaken beer as the national drink of Britain. It is now, for the first time, a billion-pound-a-year business. My postbag of wine publicity releases, which normally increases to about three or four a day in the six weeks before Christmas, was running this year at something nearer twelve to fifteen a day, with invitations to tastings and other delights in every other envelope. The world is just beginning to wake up to the huge potential market in this country: although wine consumption has doubled in recent years, we still consume only one bottle a month on average, against five bottles a week consumed in Italy.

The great bulk of the market is still in whites and lighter reds, with 70 per cent being white, just under 25 per cent being red and scarcely 6 per cent rosé. I suspect one reason why red wines have not caught on is the stupidity of marketing arrangements whereby the more expensive are far too young to drink – so that the more you pay for a red wine, the nastier it is likely to taste. With white wine, the reverse is generally the truth. I keep shouting about this, but unless the producers and wine trade generally find some way of financing the storage of wine while it matures, they will destroy the whole market in fine red wines. Practically nobody has the time or space to lay down wine for ten years or more. Until the world comes to its senses, I solemnly advise no one to pay more than £4.50 for a bottle of red wine later than 1982 – unless they are prepared to lay it down.

But the competition at the cheaper end of the market is getting fierce. I was asked to assemble my wine club panel to adjudicate between the house clarets of all the major chain stores for a wine and food programme on BBC Television. It was not a very jolly occasion. The wines were a long way down-market on the stuff we normally consider for the wine club, choice was limited to red Bordeaux which could be bought by the bottle rather than by the case, and although the Tesco's example won, none of the wines was really good enough to recommend.

A more open competition was held by the LBC wine team, which surveyed the whole field of cheapies and decided that the two best were Waitrose's Fitou Cuvée Madame Parmentier 1981 (oddly enough, I had chosen this wine for the wine club several months earlier) and Davison's Castillo Los Molines Jumilla 1979. Observe that both of these are slightly older wines. Third came an Italian white – the Sauvignon Lagedes Alto Adige 1983 (which I do not know) – and fourth the sparkling Crémant de Bourgogne from Viré, which I tasted and found most impressive at a Majestic Warehouse tasting.

My own conclusion about buying wine is that one is mad not to go to the multiples – Sainsbury's and Waitrose are the best in my experience, with Cullen's doing very well in its own area – or the warehouses (my favourite is Majestic) for ordinary drinking wine, and equally mad not to go to a serious wine merchant for the classic vintage wines of France. Waitrose has a particularly good list in the 'Other Red Wine' section, with really first-class red wines from Portugal (Fonseca's Garrafeira 1977/8), Spain (Torres Gran Coronas 1979), Australia (Berri's Cabernet-Shiraz 1982) and South Africa, not to mention Chile, California and New Zealand, and my own favourite of the lot, Hochar's Château Musar 1978 from the Lebanon. Among more conventional wines from serious wine merchants the only one I found which struck me as a quite exceptional bargain was a Château Fombrauge, St Emilion 1978 from Harvey's of Bristol. I have liked Fombrauge for some time, but this one beats the 1976 into a cocked hat and struck me as a seriously excellent wine.

Price may be a better guide to quality in claret than it is in Burgundy, but there are many pitfalls. At dinner the other evening a neighbour and friend very generously served a bottle of Château Palmer 1975 (priced in *Webster's Wine Price Guide 1986* at £34.50 to £46) followed by a bottle of Château d'Angludet 1976 (£7.50).

After making appropriate noises of wonder and delight at the Palmer we left for home, and both my wife and I remarked that the Palmer was quite remarkable in having no smell and no taste. Otherwise it was fine. The d'Angludet, by contrast, was quite delicious.

What should have been the sort of experience to tell one's grandchildren was set up by Colin Quinton of Cordier's at a lunch at l'Ecu de France in Jermyn Street, when he produced a Gruaud-Larose 1971 (£16.88 to £22.75 according to Webster), a lovely wine which faded into a single dimension when followed by the Gruaud-Larose 1953 (£110 the magnum when last seen at Christie's) and was then followed by a Gruaud-Larose 1945 (last seen at £210 the magnum). Most unfortunately, the 1945 had not quite recovered from its journey. Not to put too fine a point on it, it was all shook oop, and came out as a highly fragrant, Ribena-flavoured beetroot soup. I just wondered whether, if it *had* recovered from the journey, it would really have beaten the 1953, which was quite superb. Mr Quinton finished the meal with a beautiful, orange-coloured Sauternes tasting of peaches, apricots and honey – a Lafaurie Peyraguey 1947. There are indeed some consolations in writing about wine and mingling with these agreeable people in the trade; I feel they probably outweigh the disadvantages of being called out of bed at seven o'clock in the morning by the postman to sign for some bottles of unsolicited and almost undrinkable red wine from Cyprus.

What Hampstead Drinks Today . . .

Utterly disgusted by the wines on offer in the *Sunday Times* Wine Club Christmas promotion, I decided to conduct an investigation into what the Intelligent Thinking Man (as opposed to the ghastly New Briton who reads the *Sunday Times*) was drinking. On the principle that what Hampstead and Islington do today, Chelsea and Belgravia will be doing tomorrow (and Somerset in about five years' time), I went to see Christopher Collins whose Bibendum cash-and-carry wine store at 113 Regent's Park Road, London NW1 serves most of London's intelligentsia.

Much of his trade, he says, is taken up by Hampsteaders who turn up after work to buy wine for a dinner party that evening, often involving up to sixteen or twenty-four people. They are almost invariably having *moules marinières*, he says, followed by boeuf en croute. Twenty years ago, as I remember, it used to be a terrible tomatoey chicken dish they all served, and they drank rotten Italian wine with it, but Hampstead has got richer since then.

They still want to cut as much dash as possible with their wines for as little outlay as possible, he says, and the biggest change in fashion he has noticed has been the shift from minor clarets to Rhône wines.

The minor clarets always had the advantage not only that they were cheap but that nobody knew how minor they were. One often used to hear people saying: 'Ah yes, Château Pseudibore-Plonke', as if the name meant something to them, whereas in point of fact one knew perfectly well it was one of many thousand unclassified growths which nobody could possibly have heard of. The trouble with these minor clarets is that few of them taste very nice. One generally does better with an unattributed wine from a respectable

What Hampstead Drinks Today

négociant – like Calvet's Bordeaux Supérieur, or Médoc, or St Emilion – than one does with a pretty label and the fancy name of some non-existent château. But plain bottles do not carry quite the same cachet.

The banks of the Rhône, on the other hand, have scarcely produced any bad wine in the last twenty years. Some of its best wine, from Hermitage and Châteauneuf-du-Pape, or from Condrieu where the whites are concerned, can hold their own with the best classic wines from Burgundy and Bordeaux. They are seldom more than half the price, and often less than a quarter for their equivalent quality from these two regions.

The best wine to drink with *moules marinières* – I imagine that Hampstead's passion for this delicacy has something to do with P. G. Wodehouse's theory that molluscs and crustaceans are good for the brain – would probably be a Condrieu, but this magnificent and rare wine is not very cheap. Better than all but the most expensive grand cru white Burgundies are the Californian Chardonnays but these are creeping up the price charts now. Mr Collins has a Firestone Chardonnay 1980/81 and a Rutherford Hill, but Hampsteaders are reluctant to pay much money for anything from California which, however excellent the wine, has still to acquire snob appeal. If they were really interested in quality and nothing else they would go for the Australian Brown Bros' magnificent 1980 Chardonnay, which sells at around £6.50 and would cost something closer to £18 if it came from anywhere within ten miles of Chablis or Beaune, but nobody living north of Regent's Park can take anything from Australia seriously after Barry Humphries.

So for white wine they tend to muddle around in Alsace and northern Italy, which is now producing some impressively cheap and high-quality wines from the Tokay and Pinot Bianco grapes, usually marketed under their varietal names. Others still stick to German wines from the Rhine and, more often, Mosel, but I have the impression that the Riesling grape is falling from favour except as an aperitif in summer.

For their main red wine Mr Collins offers them a stupendous choice of Rhône reds. The best I discovered in the cheaper reaches was called Cru du Coudoulet, from the famous Beaucastel growers in Châteauneuf-du-Pape but who are presumably forbidden to use that label owing to some technicality in the immensely complicated laws of appellation contrôlée. This is a full, powerful and concentrated wine of real class. But it is very hard to go wrong in the Rhône. You pay your money and you take your choice, from the light but fruity Côtes du Ventoux, through the sturdier St Josephs to the hefty Gigondas and the Châteauneufs-du-Pape.

The king of all Rhône reds is unquestionably Hermitage, not to be confused with Crozes-Hermitage, which is seldom of the same standard.

At a recent weekend for wine buffs in the Castle Hotel, Taunton we were shown just what these Rhônes can really achieve. Starting with a Château Grillet 1971 from Condrieu, we moved on to a vertical experience of Hermitage La Chapelle – possibly the greatest name in the region – drinking wine from the vintages of 1972, 1969, 1966 and 1961. These last two were, quite simply, knock-outs. Many people present decided that they had yet to drink a premier cru of either vintage from Bordeaux which compared – and 1961 is generally agreed to have been the Bordeaux vintage of the century. One may doubt whether Hampsteaders will ever have the patience to wait as long as this. But they seem to be on the right tracks.

Aperitifs

Aperitifs are not to be confused with aperients, which are laxatives designed to open the bowels, as nurses invariably explain. Aperitifs are intended to whet or sharpen the appetite for food. They also fill the empty hours between noon and luncheon, between six o'clock in the evening and dinner time which, in the age of hostess–cooks, may be delayed until 9.30 or even later. I have noticed that male university students (or undergraduates, as they used to be called in the days when everybody went to Oxford) often call for Guinness or beer at these times of day. There is no reason why they should not be given these things, which are slightly cheaper, in any case, than most other drinks, but they should not be encouraged to suppose that this indulgence is part of the polite convention discussed here. The effect of beer may be to fill them out and give them a more manly figure – I have been told that the beer-belly is sexually irresistible to many women in the north of England, where they call it a 'corporation', implying wealth and power – but it is no good pretending that beer sharpens the appetite for food.

Nor do cocktails, except possibly a dry Martini cocktail, served straight up with a twist of lemon skin squeezed over for flavouring. The general effect of cocktails is to anaesthetise the brain, drive out the worries and preoccupations of the day and prepare men and women for each other's company. This is not at all the same thing as whetting the appetite for luncheon or dinner. The purpose of an aperitif is definitely not to make one drunk. This should come with the wine or, failing that, with the port and other delights afterwards. Even so, this does not solve the problem of what to do in the difficult time between six o'clock, when the nation may be assumed to have returned from work, and 8.30 or even later when it sits down to dinner. Many workers feel the need to get drunk – or at any rate to anaesthetise the brain – in that time. In my parents' time, when people still changed for dinner, they would drink cocktails or whisky to make themselves drunk between 6.00 and about 7.45, then retire to change for dinner and on their reappearance at 8.00 or 8.15 they would be offered a glass of sherry as an aperitif.

Sherry is still the most generally acceptable aperitif, but one cannot drink it all evening without the most appalling effects. Two glasses should be the maximum, taken just before a meal. It is boring to say so, but I have yet to discover any more reliable sherries than Gonzalez Byass's Tio Pepe or Domecq's Fino La Ina, both at the top end of the market. Others swear by fancy products with dressing-gown cord tassels attached called Garvey's San Patricio, but my own favourite fino is Harvey's Isabelita, almost impossible to find unless you are prepared to order it direct from Harvey's. The greatest horror and shame is when people decide they cannot afford Tio Pepe and buy Gonzalez Byass's Elegante instead. It looks much the same but tastes truly disgusting to the sherry drinker. The only good cheap sherries I have found are Sainsbury's Manzanilla and Harvey's Luncheon Dry.

For those who insist on long or fizzy drinks and do not wish to get drunk on gin and tonic or whisky and soda, there are sherry and white port mixers available in addition to the range of spritzers – what used to be called hock-and-seltzer, regardless of the wine from which it was made. Taylor, currently judged the best name in port, produces a white port specially for mixing with tonic called Chip Dry, while Cockburn suggest their Fine Old White Port for this purpose. They also suggest mixing it with lemonade. Perhaps the younger generation would like this. I have tried none of them, but Harvey's special mixer sherry, called Tico, is much less disgusting than it sounds when mixed with tonic.

The spritzer, which started life as hock and soda, is now made from any strong-tasting cheap white wine, with or without a dash of orange or peach bitters (these are almost unprocurable outside Amsterdam. Angostura is good, too). Try your grocer's Muscadet, or any of the stronger varietals from northern Italy – Pinot Grigio or Tocai from my energetic bachelor friend Colin Price-Beech at Recount Wines.

These wines, with the Pinot Bianco and Chardonnay, are good enough to drink alone as an aperitif. The latter two, being slightly sharper, may also be used for Kir. Nearly all wine merchants now sell the blackcurrant liqueur, Kir or crème de cassis, for making this drink, but if they charge over £6.00 I should use Ribena and brandy: one part Ribena to two parts cooking brandy to twenty parts white wine. It is pretty foul but people knock it back. Generally speaking, I feel an aperitif should not be seen as a thirst-quencher. If you are thirsty, drink tea, then move on.

Almost any white wine serves very well as an aperitif so long as you like it. The best thing is to decide which grape variety you like best and then go for your own price range. Muscadet, being so cheap, is immensely popular nowadays, but much Muscadet is too harsh to drink without food. The best I have yet discovered is the Sauvion range from Le Nez Rouge and the best medium-priced one in that range is called Domaine du Bois-Curé. Otherwise, I should tend to leave Muscadet alone as an aperitif.

As for German wines, almost any Kabinett or Spätlese makes a good aperitif. Slightly smarter nowadays, because more laid back, is the Alsatian range: Sylvaner (the cheapest but not bad at all), Riesling, rather drier than its German equivalents, the best and spiciest Gewürztraminer in the world (I have yet to find any better than the Hugel range, available from Berry Bros and many others), not to mention Pinot Blanc (can be sharpish), Pinot Gris (mysteriously called Tokay) and a dry Muscat, which tastes like a Beaumes de Venise without the sweetness, if you can imagine that. I am not sure who is the best specialist on Alsatian wines, never having investigated them in depth, but I observe that O. W. Loeb has all these varietals. They are never particularly cheap but they are all (apart perhaps from the Sylvaner) considered exceptionally elegant.

For those who like the Chardonnay grape, it is mad to serve an expensive white Burgundy as an aperitif. Try a petit Chablis – Marks and Spencer have a very decent one – or any of the excellent 1983 Mâcon Villages in any decent chain store at the same sort of price. The most characteristic Sauvignon taste comes not from Bordeaux but from the Loire, the Sancerres and Pouilly Fumé, but I judge them slightly sharp for an aperitif.

Finally, there is the whole range of vermouths, which should generally be served with ice and slices of lemon to keep up with the television advertisements. Perhaps I shall write separately about them, although I feel one soon gets pretty fed up with any particular one. Chambery (Sainsbury's provide a perfectly good example) was thought smart at one time – until, perhaps, it reached Sainsbury's – and it is certainly less disgusting than sweet white Martini and Cinzano Bianco, let alone their appalling new rosés. But really the best aperitif in the world is champagne.

Dessert Wines

Sweet wines have been made for as long as wine has been known. In fairly recent history they were drunk throughout a meal by people who saw nothing wrong in the idea of a mouthful of sugar to accompany their roast beef. After all, we eat redcurrant jelly with roast lamb (although the French rather laugh at us for this) as well as sweet mint sauce; we think nothing of serving apple sauce with pork, cranberry sauce with turkey, or cooked ham, or venison. So in Germany, among the traditional classes, it is still perfectly normal to drink an Auslese or even a Bierenauslese (very sweet indeed) throughout the meal.

Nowadays we wine buffs rather shudder at the idea of drinking a rich golden Sauternes with roast meat, but I think we are wrong. Among less sophisticated wine-drinkers – including most of this year's million-and-a-half new drinkers – the taste is for sweeter wine, although not yet for wine as sweet as the great dessert wines we shall be discussing. The great increase is in semi-sweet white Common Market blended wine, mostly produced in Germany. It is a sad fact about writing on wine that for the vast majority of wine-drinkers in this country, their idea of heaven is Sichel's Blue Nun Liebfraumilch – not as nasty, to my taste, as some of these new Common Market blends, but certainly on the way there.

I have been told that a famous branded wine-maker, once known for his Beaujolais and Mâconnais, now owned by a British concern, was researching the British market for the ideal red wine suitable for mass consumption. A vox populi wine-tasting was held among volunteers dragged from the street or from the proverbial Clapham omnibus. The red wine they voted the best was something they had made specially for the occasion – Blue Nun Liebfraumilch with cochineal added for colouring.

One hopes, as a wine-writer, one day to lure the British mass market away from this depraved taste for semi-sweet wine, but the simple truth is that most people like it, and insist on finding the magnificent red wines of Bordeaux and Burgundy too sharp for their taste. I wonder if they might be led back to the straight and narrow path by exposure to the *really* sweet dessert wines of France, Germany and Hungary. For some reason – chiefly, I suspect, because they are too expensive to please the new generation of wine-drinkers at their present state of involvement in wine – they have never caught on. But there is a logical development from these foul Deutsche Tafelweins and Liebfraumilchs through the slightly sweeter and more expensive Spätleses to the Ausleses, Bierenausleses and Trockenbierenausleses – made from specially selected shrivelled grapes of an indescribable sweetness. Once a taste for really good wine has been acquired, it will never be lost.

There are important great sweet white wines in the world, by my reckoning, and three of them come from France. King of them all is the great golden wine of Sauternes and Barsac, south-east of Bordeaux. This is made from the Sémillon grape, and although the Australians have used Sémillon to make some excellent dry white wines, nobody else has yet succeeded in making a really good sweet one. The very best Sauternes, Château d'Yquem, is now so expensive that it has become a joke, but the other first-rank châteaux – Rieussec, Suduiraut, Climens, Coutet, Guiraud – are much cheaper and very nearly as good. A really good year – the best recent ones are 1967, 1970, 1976 and possibly 1983, although this last will need keeping at least seven years – will produce brilliant wine from the minor châteaux, and these can be very cheap. All serious wine merchants have a range of these wines. Cheapest of all is a near-Sauternes called Cérons, of which a reasonable example can be had from the IECS Wine Society.

The great problem with Sauternes (and Barsac, Cérons, etc.) is when to drink it. Normal practice nowadays is to serve them at the end of the meal with the pudding. It is true that very few wines go with pudding, except champagne, but I have always found – and a growing body of wine-drinkers now agree with me – that an intensely sweet pudding completely spoils Sauternes by taking all the sweetness out of it, so that one might as well be drinking a dry

Dessert Wines

wine. The whole point of Sauternes is its ravishing, luscious sweetness. Some French people drink it only with foie gras, but to my mind this spoils the subtle taste of the foie gras. In my experience, Sauternes is best drunk at the end of a meal with fruitcake, nuts or mild cheese – butter does not spoil it – or with fresh fruit. It should never be drunk with sugary, jammy confections, or even with anything as sweet as pineapple. One glass of it – not more – before lunch makes an excellent aperitif.

The years I mentioned as the best in Sauternes are those which produced a significant amount of noble rot (*Botrytis cinerea*) in the grape. This is when a sunny, dry but misty autumn causes the grapes to shrivel so that the sugar is concentrated. The same effect is pursued with Teutonic zeal on the banks of the Rhine and the Mosel, which provide the second important group of sweet wines. Most German wine of the sort sold by the gallon in Britain has masses of sugar added. The better wines of the better years do not, and it is to these one should turn. In fact 1983 was the first good year in Germany since 1976, which was a very small vintage, so they are only beginning to appear on the market.

There are those who go for the Riesling grape and those who don't. My own kindest thought about it is that at its very best and most expensive, it begins to taste like Sauternes. German wines are a special subject understood only by a few, but where the rich, luscious wines are concerned quality control is so strict that nobody can go seriously wrong. Every wine is graded by its natural sugar content; it is unnecessary to know anything about vintages, since natural sugar content is the decisive factor, being determined by the ripeness of grapes at harvest. In ascending order of sweetness (and price) the grades are: Kabinett, Spätlese, Auslese, Beerenauslese, Trockenbeerenauslese. These last are both very rare and very expensive indeed. Beware of imitations – especially from Austria. The Austrians have taken to writing 'Trockenbeerenauslese' in large letters all over any old sugared-up table wine, but the price gives them away. If anyone really wishes to take an interest in these sweet German dessert wines they should ask advice from one or other of the specialist wine merchants (Loeb and Hallgarten). So few people in this country are interested in the better German wines that they are not very expensive, at any rate in the middle ranges.

The third group of sweet wines comes from the Loire. These are made from the Chenin Blanc grape, also used around Anjou to make disgusting sweet 'n' sour table wine, although the South Africans have developed a respectable dry white wine from it. The best come from the Coteaux du Layon – Bonnezeaux and Quarts de Chaume – and have a high acid content in addition to intense sweetness. They should be kept for years and years, which practically nobody in Britain is prepared to do. At their best, they are memorable, and no sweet wine freak should miss out on them. But the only wine merchant I know who keeps a stock of old Bonnezeaux, as well as the young stuff, is Robin Yapp of Mere.

Finally from France, there are the wines made from the Muscat grape, of which the Muscat de Beaumes de Venise has taken Britain by storm in the last few years. This is so scented and over-powering in its grapiness that until recently women spurned it as a tarts' tipple and men feared for their manliness. Anybody who has ever eaten a Muscatel dessert grape will recognise the taste immediately. Nobody can possibly dislike it, although some of the cheaper examples cloy after a bit. The best one widely available is from Vidal Fleury, but Bibendum sometimes also has an even better one from the Domaine de Beaucastel. The rarest and snobbiest is called Domaine Durban, sold by Corney and Barrow, but cheap examples from the Caves Co-opératives have been available at Sainsbury's. Beaumes is highly alcoholic, being slightly fortified, and is not really for serious wine-drinkers, but it is absolutely delicious and beats all the other Muscats of France and the world (except for a rare example made by J. Fonseca in Setubal, Portugal) into a cocked hat.

Last of all what should be the grandest of the lot, the drink of emperors and archdukes, Hungary's Imperial Tokay. I have never really seen the point of it, but it has to be mentioned. Made from the Furmint grape, whatever that may be, Tokay comes from Hungary's Russian border and is carefully graded, along the German model, according to how much *Aszu* of botrytis-ridden sweet concentrate it has in it. The highest score is six *puttonyos*, but I have never tasted that. Hugh Johnson compares it, at its best, to an oxidised Sauternes. Berry Bros and Rudd sell a 1975 five-*puttonyos* example. I was never a Russian emperor or an archduke of Austria, but at least the modern age allows us all to give the feeling a try.

Summer Wines

Much unnecessary suffering is caused by the theory that you have to drink whites and rosés in summer. In fact much summer food – and in particular cold meat – is crying out for a hefty red. White wine is just as alcoholic as red and probably makes one rather drunker as one tends to drink more of it. It is all a load of rubbish. I think red wine may also be better for suntans, feeding the melanin pigment. But the important thing about summer wines is that they tend to be cheaper than the winter ones. Classic wines of Bordeaux, Burgundy and the Rhône are left quietly maturing in the cellars as their owners frisk and frolic on the beach. And there can be no doubt that many white and most rosé wines are best when drunk out of doors.

The main thing about cheap wine is that it is easy to find pleasant slurping stuff in any chain store, so long as it does not have much taste. As soon as cheap wine develops a taste, it divides pretty sharply into those wines you find disgusting and those which you personally find quite delicious. It is a very personal thing, this cheap wine. The closest friends can disagree violently. But it is a good idea to devote this section to cheap wines for summer drinking, starting with a house wine with many of the characteristics of southern Burgundy, although it has no appellation. I first heard of Grand Vernaux Vin de Table Rouge from a friend in Fleet Street, who swore he would never drink anything else. It is quite easily the best bargain I have discovered for several years. To all intents and purposes it is a full, fat Burgundy – perhaps slightly sweet for the purist, but without any of the thin, sharp, mean taste of many minor Burgundies. It comes from an Oxford firm called Grape Ideas and carries my strongest possible recommendation as a drink for summer evenings.

Summer Wines

For luncheon in summer, when eaten indoors (as most of our summer luncheons are eaten, whatever we might like to remember), one of the best possible drinks is a lightly chilled Beaujolais, but I can't be bothered to go through the Beaujolais routine on this occasion. Find one you like and chill it. A much cheaper variation on Beaujolais, made from the same grape, would be a Gamay de l'Ardèche, from central France. This area is chiefly famous for its Syrah, which I personally find rather disgusting. Both examples are available from Wineheads. The same firm offers an extremely elegant alternative to Beaujolais in a St-Nicolas de Bourgueil from the distinguished grower Max Talman. Bourgueil, for those who have never discovered it on their way through France, is the most delicious of all the Loire reds – light, zippy and full of taste – which should also be served slightly chilled.

So much for the summer reds, although before leaving them I might mention that a huge selection of very cheap wines from the Languedoc is available from Lavinia Gibbs-Smith. I have never found a single decent white wine in the Languedoc (unless one counts Provence, where the Domaine de la Rouillère, near St Tropez, is at last beginning to make itself felt on the English market) but the reds offer a wide choice, and anyone who 'discovered' a particular wine on holiday in the area may well find it on the Gibbs-Smith list.

Where pink wine is concerned I am convinced that nothing beats Tavel and it is a waste of time messing around with anything from further north. Avoid in particular anything from Anjou. Oddly enough, I remember the time when the disgusting Portuguese Mateus Rosé was a perfectly decent wine, but then I remember when Big Ben was the size of a pocket-watch.

Where summer whites are concerned, I generally advise people to avoid the cheaper German (or Alsatian, let alone Yugoslav) Rieslings. A tremendous amount of unnecessary suffering goes on under the name of Liebfraumilch. Of course there are some excellent Rieslings to be bought, but they are not particularly cheap. For those readers who are still old-fashioned enough to smoke pot, the only wine I ever found which went well with it was Deinhart's Hochheimer Konigin Victoria Beng Riesling Kabinett. This is a particularly good wine which also carries a beautiful picture of Queen Victoria on the label, which seemed vaguely suitable.

Some of the great bargains in white wine come from northern Italy. A wide choice of Chardonnays, Pinot Grigios and Pinot Biancos is available from my enterprising friend Colin Price-Beech and also from Simon Loftus of Adnams.

Finally, spare a thought for the former colonies. Paul Masson (chiefly famous in this country for his indifferent jug wines) produces a really excellent Chardonnay. And Cullen's offer an interesting South African white – KWV's Cape Foret, which is worth a try for those who have never discovered South African wines.

All these wines are more chic, as well as cheaper, than third-rate Chablis, and a great deal better than any of the supermarket house wines which people buy in two-litre flasks, thinking they may save money.

FRANCE

Burgundy Now and Then

I wonder if I am alone among serious wine-buyers and drinkers in suspecting that there is a conspiracy in the trade, aided and abetted by wine-writers and 'experts' with trade connections, to bully us into buying whatever they have to sell. If such a conspiracy exists, it is almost certainly unspoken and might even flourish beneath the conscious awareness of the conspirators. Nor is it confined to Burgundy. My first mistake was to be taken in by all the hype for the 1975 port vintage. I bought cases and cases on expert assurances that it would be the vintage of the century. When the 1977 vintage came round, I initially felt that the trade had called 'wolf' once too often, and so had to buy what undoubtedly will prove to be a major vintage much more expensively later on. Where claret is concerned, I observe with amazement that Alexis Lichine in his edition of *Encyclopaedia of Wines and Spirits* awards the 1984 vintage seventeen out of a possible twenty points – exactly the same high score as he awards to such excellent vintages as 1959 and 1971. Now I have not tasted any of the 1984 red Bordeaux yet, and I suppose it is possible that Mr Lichine may be right. But I am also aware that 1984 marked the virtual failure of the Merlot grape, that wines will be thrown out of their traditional balance as a result, and that other experts, who *have* tasted the wines and are not connected with the trade, have discussed the vintage in terms of another 1972, which will burst the claret price bubble yet again. But of course the trade must sell these 1984 red Bordeaux somehow. Private wine-buyers (not to mention Business Expansion Schemes) will not find out their mistake, if it is a mistake, for at least five years, by which time some really good vintages will have come along which people will be queuing up to buy at any price they ask...

Where Burgundy is concerned, the conspiracy may have gone even further. I was touched and moved to read in a book by Don Hewitson, the extrovert New Zealander (*Enjoying Wine*), that he has had exactly the same experience as I have. Writing about his memories of the 1960s, he says

> there were the unparalleled joys of enjoying reasonably priced attractive, rich and luscious burgundies. A dinner time bottle of common-place Côte de Beaune-Villages would ease the worries of the business day: now all a similar bottle does is make me annoyed (at the thinness and lack of fruit) and resentful (if I have paid out sufficient money to buy a couple of bottles of excellent drinking claret or Beaujolais).

One explanation could be that Hewitson and I have faulty memories. However, as a third 'jilted lover of red burgundy' – Howard Ripley – points out, it is still possible to find exactly the same wine as we remember, here and there, although neither the year, nor the commune, nor the vineyard on the label provides sufficient guidance to identify such wines. A famous lady wine expert – who certainly knows twenty times as much as I do on the subject – told me at lunch recently that what she particularly enjoyed about Burgundy was identifying the particular character of each commune – whether Volnay, Chambolle, Santenay or what you will – and then proceeding to guess the vineyard. My own experience of the wine world suggests that this is an absurdity. Not only do the communes have no identifiable characteristics – in the sense that the range of wines in each is too big to make any generalisations useful – but even within one vineyard, frequently shared between twenty or thirty growers, you get vines of all ages, some well pruned and producing a beautiful, rich intense wine which might have come from a grand cru of the 1950s, others unpruned, over-fertilised and producing a pale, thin red wine smelling of raw meat which might have come from Sancerre on the Loire. In a big climat like Clos de Vougeot, shared between over a hundred growers, many producing their own wine in their own way, and with a huge variety of sub-soils in a tiny area, it is possible to find wines of the same year coming from adjoining patches of land which are as different as chalk from cheese.

The result is that it is almost impossible to be knowledgeable about Burgundy. While it is comparatively easy to learn about the châteaux and vintages of Bordeaux, there is no equivalent store of knowledge to be had about the myriad growers of Burgundy. As Anthony Hanson makes plain in his authoritative treatise *Burgundy*: 'There is absolutely no substitute for tasting what is in the bottle.'

Mr Hanson knows as much about Burgundy as any man alive. He certainly knows twenty times as much as I do, just as Mr Alexis Lichine knows about a hundred times as much as I do about claret, which did not prevent him from awarding the 1984 Bordeaux seventeen points out of twenty. In fact it added to his authority in making this assessment. The fact that Mr Hanson may be connected with the trade did not prevent him from publishing one of the savagest attacks on declining standards in the area which I have ever read, when he wrote about 'mediocre wines without quality and poor value for money. Briefly, a rip-off. The Burgundians are coasting along on their reputation.' This judgement was endorsed by David Wolfe after a recent tasting of Gevrey-Chambertins, where he decided there was not a single wine on offer which he would have bought: 'The general malaise of Burgundy may be summed up as a startling disparity between quality and price.' In other words, the limited quantity of red wine which Burgundy can produce – I do not propose to discuss white Burgundy here, since it is an entirely different subject – is so oversubscribed as a result of people's memories of how Burgundy used to taste that the growers can sell their products no matter how silly and thin they taste now.

My point is that Mr Hanson is plainly an honest man, just as Mr Lichine is plainly an honest man. Mr Hanson is also someone who has to sell whatever Burgundy he can buy, having decided that it is the best on offer. In the present circumstances of the wine trade this means that he has to sell it as soon as it comes in – possibly two or three years after the grapes are gathered and pressed. From my memory of twenty-five to thirty years ago, one was practically never offered respectable Burgundy before it was at least six years in bottle. The pressure on wine-growers to produce quick-maturing wine, drinkable after two or three years, has never been greater, but in fact no process has yet been discovered which will have the same effect on wine as ageing in bottle. If the growers can sell their wine without ageing it there is no reason for them to age it; if the wine merchants are unable to age their wine as a result of financial constrictions, they must somehow persuade the public to buy immature wine and pretend it is ready for drinking, since very few wine-drinkers have either the space or the patience to lay down wine for eight or nine years (let alone the twenty-five or so years needed by some of the best clarets and ports) and in many cases they may be doubtful of the necessary life expectancy.

The conspiracy within the wine trade thus takes two forms: on growers to produce dilute wines in large quantities, insufficiently vatted, to make quick and easy drinking; and on merchants to pretend at the same time that these thin, pale Burgundies are what the wine should really taste like, or alternatively (now the consumers are getting wise to this trick) that Burgundies made properly according to the instructions of Napoleon's Minister of Agriculture, Jean Chaptal, in 1801 – he is the father of what is now called traditional Burgundy – may be drunk within a few years of vintage.

Chaptal's instructions, as Mr Hanson pointed out in his learned and informative article 'Burgundy Then and Now' in *Christie's Wine Companion*, permitted the addition of sugar and boiling must and prescribed a weighted cover on floating grape skins in the vat to allow maximum infusion of tannin – the recipe for a slow-maturing wine of great density. They were also interpreted to allow the 'beefing up' of thin vintages by addition of coarse young Rhône and Midi wines and, for the English market, brandy and even port.

Obviously such blending or 'beefing up' required enormous skill. Over-sugaring produced a wine which was either too alcoholic or too sweet, over-vatting produced a wine which was excessively raw and tannic, over-blending produced a wine which lacked any of the characteristic excellences or subtlety of the Pinot grape. The extent to which these practices are now regarded as heretical – some of them are even illegal – is illustrated by the way that the word 'chaptalised', deriving from Napoleon's blameless Minister of Agriculture, is now used almost exclusively to denote a wine which has been over-sugared or over-cooked. Yet it was these practices which produced, year after year, the splendid wines which Don Hewitson remembers, wines which can still be found at auction, usually in English bottlings by Berry Bros, Avery's of Bristol or British Railways. The best ones needed ten to fifteen years in bottle and lived for anything up to another ten years after that.

Mr Hanson, in his article in *Christie's Wine Companion*, mentioned that for the first 1,350 years or so of its existence as a wine-producing area, Burgundy produced a light, fast-maturing wine. It was only in the nineteenth century that longer vatting time and Mr Chaptal's other remedies started producing the deep, intense wines we grew to know and love in England. He suggests that this English taste may be some form of perversion, like our national taste for being whipped. I remember once, in a flight of fancy, describing a Burgundy I was offering to members of the *Spectator* Wine Club, which I organise, as 'anal'. Left-wingers and progressives will be delighted to learn that it was a sell-out.

But the argument that early practices must hold some greater validity than those which emerged from the wonderful cauldron of intellectual and scientific discovery which was the nineteenth century simply won't do. One hears the same arguments advanced in liturgical discussion: that the Early Christians always used to play guitars, embrace each other and share buns together at their impromptu love-feasts which preceded the formalised ceremonies of Eucharist or Mass. It is all a load of rubbish. Tradition and conservatism are bound to embrace whatever is useful in the process of change or development, as well as fighting the good fight against harmful change. I can well understand that it would be much more convenient for the wine trade if we could be persuaded to accept Burgundy as a light, fast-maturing wine. But consumers must learn to resist this suggestion and stamp on it whenever it is made. Wine merchants should be joining the battle on their behalf against the growers and producers, not taking their side. If a tiny proportion of the Common Agricultural Policy funds paid to wine-makers in the Midi for producing millions of gallons of undrinkable wine for the wine lake was devoted to encouraging serious producers to age their wine before sale, the world would be a happier and saner place.

One began to suspect that Mr Hanson was arguing a case rather than writing from the heart when he started quoting ancient authors in his attempt to prove that Burgundy was and should be a light, quick-maturing wine. Being an honest man, he also supplied us with all the ammunition needed to knock down his arguments: thus the reason Burgundy was formerly a paler wine was not over-production, as now, but that a large proportion of white grapes was included. When he quoted Cyrus Redding, in 1851, as reckoning that a bottle of Burgundy peaked after two years, he also recorded Mr Redding's impression that Chambolle was in the Côte de Beaune, Vosne Romanée in the Côte Challonaise, adding weakly that Mr Redding at least gave the impression of having gathered his facts at first hand. I am surprised that he did not pick up Shakespeare's reference in *King Lear* where the King of France says: 'Not all the Dukes of waterish Burgundy shall take this unprized, precious maid from me.'

But it won't do. Perhaps not many Burgundy lovers have allowed themselves to be brainwashed, but the evil influence of the wine investors, who treat fine wine like rare postage stamps, as entries in a ledger of commodities rather than as something which anybody is going to drink, allows the famous producers to put any rubbish into their bottles so long as it has a famous label and an 'approved' year. I would like to think that the bottom is going to fall out of this market when the Business Expansion Schemes start selling their 'investments' in four years' time. At present the only bargains to be found in Burgundy are among the parcels of old English-bottled Burgundies at auction, and the only worthwhile new Burgundies among a tiny band of traditional producers. Remoissenet has never disappointed me, Doudet-Naudin very seldom, and I was delighted to discover among the 1983 tastings that Moillard seems to have seen the light. I wish I could say the same for Clair-Daü, Drouhin or even Jadot. But investors are having as bad an effect on Burgundy as phylloxera ever did, and until one can convince the world that Romanée Conti is a wine rather than an investment bond, the future is very bleak.

Buyers and Cellars

1984 seems to have been a wash-out throughout most of France. Wine-buyers will now be scrambling for what they can find from the annus mirabilis of 1983, when every major wine area seems to have excelled.

Most merchants have sent out their 1983 Burgundy opening offers. Before very long, the 1983 Burgundies will all have arrived in this country and will be featuring in the ordinary retail lists of those merchants who still take Burgundy seriously, at whatever exalted price they choose.

Although 1983 was a classic year for wines, the reds now taste hard, austere, often with no trace of residual sugar and a massive tannic back-bite which makes one wonder if they have been mistaking their chemicals and adding caustic soda instead of the traditional antifreeze. Tasting them is an extraordinarily unpleasant experience. Only the trained palate – and one which earns its livelihood from suffering in this way – can discern the quality underneath. After nearly six months of tasting these wines, I think I am getting the hang of them. But to read the wine merchants' descriptions – 'full rich round early palate and good depth of flavour in the middle; pleasant soft tannin finish gives good balance. Full flavour and already showing some complexity' – punters might suppose they will be buying themselves a pleasant drink. Nothing could be further from the truth. They will find themselves drinking substances which citizens of a free country should never be called upon to know about, tasting of liquid zinc, mulberry leaves, over-infused tea and old penknives. Those who are gulled into drinking them now will probably never buy expensive Burgundy again.

Since I regard these 1983 Burgundies as one of the most serious topics for discussion of the decade – if not *the* most serious – I will proceed to discuss them, but I must make it plain, after the above warning, that my remarks are addressed only to people who are serious wine-drinkers, Burgundians who are prepared to spend large sums of money on wine they will not drink for at least ten years *and* who have both the storage space and life expectancy to make the enterprise worthwhile. Those with less patience should concentrate on the 1982s, of which a very good selection was shown by Heyman Brothers. The one I bought was an Aloxe-Corton from Tollot-Beaut. Other excellent examples were a Savigny Les Lavières from Chandon de Briailles, a magnificently deep Volnay Santenots from Jacques Prieur, a richly anal Volnay Verseuil from Clerget, and a beautifully scented Gevrey-Chambertin from Armand Rousseau. Of the more expensive but less interesting 1982 Burgundies, two Nuits St-Georges – Les Pruliers and Les Vaucrains, both from Henri Gouges – excited me. They both had the thick, sweet, deep taste one associates with the old-fashioned style of Burgundy.

Now for the 1983s. Their problem, as I have said, is that they are nearly all too disgusting to think about now, but I honestly believe we should all buy as much as we can afford since there are some magnificent wines here struggling to emerge in ten to fifteen years' time. For once I have put my money where my mouth is, ordering thirteen cases from Avery's of Bristol, and innumerable odd cases all over the place. With their help (and that of the 1977 and 1983 ports) I hope to face a happy and contented old age.

Since, as I say, I did not really trust my own judgement in sorting out these horrible liquids, my method was to go through the twenty-two red Burgundies on Avery's opening offer of 1983, picking out those which John Avery had described as either 'rich' or 'almost sweet'. These are the qualities I look for in Burgundy. Stuff 'elegance', a euphemism for thinness; 'muscularity', which means coarseness; 'subtlety', which, at this early stage, means tastelessness. Stuff, above all, the 'modern fruity flavoury style'. The interesting thing about my Avery order is that I chose them untasted, reckoning that John Avery was about the best judge of Burgundy in England and he had never let me down in the past. In about twelve years' time I will know whether or not my childlike faith was justified.

Buyers and Cellars

As for the innumerable 1983 Burgundies I *have* tasted in the course of the summer, I should say that the only important generalisation to be made, which is true of nearly all Burgundy these days, is that quality bears very little relationship to price or label. Avoid anything from Pommard; I have yet to find a good 1983 Vougeot – and treat most of the grands crus with suspicion, except Corton.

Of all the tastings I attended, I was most disappointed by the Louis Jadot range. I do not know why, but Jadot – normally among the top four or five of the big Burgundy négociants – does not seem to have been performing well this year. In a huge range, I did not find a single wine I wanted to buy at its price. The pleasantest surprise came from the house of Moillard, whose name I associate with some shocking 1976s (they tell me the 1977s are better, which is worth knowing) and a generally light, modern style. However, with their modern techniques they have tried a new method and produced spectacular results. Here are notes on my three favourites:

1 Les Vignes Hautes, Hautes Côtes de Nuits. One would expect a light wine with such a label, but this one is full of fruit.

2 Nuits St-Georges Clos de Thorey. A lovely, full, uncomplicated wine, deep in colour with a rich, sweet smell.

3 Corton Clos des Vergennes. Rich nose, creamy and burned. Wonderful sweet, heavy taste.

Of the other négociants, some of whose 1983s will not be drinkable for ten years, I had better hold my peace. My best advice is to find a wine merchant you trust and buy, buy, buy.

Quaff Beaujolais Quickly

Beaujolais – with the exception of the heaviest grands crus from Moulin-à-Vent, which should really be treated as Burgundy – must never be left in the glass for more than a few minutes. Nothing happens to it through exposure to air but deterioration and collapse. An open bottle should never be left between meals; if it is left overnight it tastes cheap and sour next day. It should be drunk as soon as it is opened, straight through until the bottle is finished, and served cool but not cold.

The best Beaujolais is bottled in France, since it travels better in bottle than in cask. The only exception to this rule which I can think of is the Moulin-à-Vent shipped by Berry Bros. Their Morgon 1978 is slightly thinner and we are talking more about a Burgundy-style wine than a Beaujolais. The only Beaujolais-style Beaujolais I have found which sometimes retains its fresh Gamay taste after bottling in England is the Wine Society's Beaujolais Villages. This is good in a good year, bad in a bad year.

The great lesson of Beaujolais is that labels provide only a rough indication of what you are going to find inside. The thing to do is to find one you like and then order dozens and dozens of it before stocks are exhausted, which they usually are pretty fast.

Never buy anything which is just called Beaujolais, without further description, until you have tasted it, as it is usually (but not always) pretty poor stuff. Nowadays it always comes from the right area, but this is no guarantee that it will be any better than tinned Hirondelle. The main bargains are to be found among the Villages.

As far as drinking the Primeur or Beaujolais Nouveau on 15 November is concerned, nothing tastes at its best after it has been carried on the back of a Hell's Angel's motorbike for 500 miles or tied to an SAS hero's legs and parachuted into the Thames.

In any case, the Beaujolais supplied on these occasions is usually pretty good muck. It is just an excuse for a lot of repressed businessmen to get drunk on a Monday morning. At my age I am more interested in the new pleasure I have discovered in Taunton called horizontal tasting...

Quaff Beaujolais Quickly

Dry White Bordeaux

Dry white Bordeaux has never enjoyed much of a reputation in Britain. Various explanations are offered for this. The simplest one, advanced by young Nicholas Davies of the Hungerford Wine Company, is that it always used to taste pretty nasty – either over-sulphured and far from fresh or abominably acidic. In fact, with very few exceptions, these wines were usually produced by wine-makers to give their workers in place of the more highly-prized red wines, which they could sell. It was only with the rise in the value of vineyard space in the region – and the easy availability of cheap imported or French wine lake plonk to give their workers – that they started cultivating their white wine grapes and making an effort with their production.

But tastes have been slow to catch up with the vastly improved white wines now available from Bordeaux, with the result that they are still extraordinarily cheap for their quality, if one chooses with care. Another problem, according to Mr Davies, is that there is still an enormous amount of rubbish on the market – sugared-up stuff from Entre-Deux-Mers and even Graves, describing itself as 'medium' and making a doomed attempt to catch the established taste among lower-middle-class English wine-drinkers for sugared-up German filth called Liebfraumilch.

Many wine merchants, when asked about dry white Bordeaux, still tend to curl their opulent lips and hand you over to their assistant. Some, however, like the immensely experienced royal warrant-holders Corney and Barrow, have long made a speciality of dry white Bordeaux (among other things) and I found a number of keen, younger merchants who were most anxious to increase their lists and persuade people of its new excellence. The result was that a mystifying twenty-six sample bottles arrived from six wine merchants, and I had to arrange a series of tastings among trusted neighbours.

Colin Price-Beech, of Recount Wines, attributes the great improvement in white Bordeaux wine-making to a process of cold fermentation which the French have just learned from the Italians. It is true that the process seems to give these wines a fresh, zingy quality at the cheaper end of the market which they earlier lacked. But Nicholas Davies attributes it to greater use of the Sauvignon grape, pushing out the buttery roundness of the Sémillon (which is chiefly used to make the sweet dessert wines of Sauternes and Barsac). As if to prove them both wrong one observes that the winners at both ends of the price scale have very high Sémillon ratings – the Château du Juge has 50 per cent, and the extraordinary Château Laville–Haut-Brion, most expensive of all dry whites, has 40 per cent, and is produced by the traditional methods.

The truth is that one can make no hard and fast rules about what sort of dry white Bordeaux is liable to be best. The only thing to do is taste as many as possible and mark down the best. That is the humble function of a wine correspondent.

The winner in the cheapest class was generally agreed to be the Château du Juge 1982. It is an amazingly good wine, imported from Sichel and available from Cullen's. After the Château du Juge we passed fairly quickly through Cordier's two house wines – the Blanc Bordeaux and the Graves, available from Les Amis du Vin and Winefare – as being respectable table wines but a little dead by the standards already set. Similarly an Entre-Deux-Mers 1982 from Harvey's called Château La Réunion was obviously a decent example at a fair price, but nothing to rave about. Up a bit in price, and the good wines started coming thick and fast.

First a Château le Peuy Saincrit from the Hungerford Wine Company, then a Château du Rey from the same source. There is an excellently light, fresh Graves from Victoria Wines. Next Haynes Hanson's Château Montalivet (Graves). For a few pence more, you have a really full and fruity wine from Harvey's called Château Bellevue.

At this point you move into the fairly expensive and serious dry white Bordeaux, which are something quite different. The experts here are undoubtedly Corney and Barrow. Tastes differ quite markedly, and it is simply not true that the more you pay, the more you are going to like it. I can only suggest that in this range you try for yourself - between Corney and Barrow's highly scented Doisy-Daëne 1981 and their slightly sharper La Tuilerie 1982. Before moving to the classics, I might mention Cordier's Château du Magnum. This one slips down very easily indeed, and I was not at all surprised to learn that it had been chosen by the Roux brothers for their restaurants at Le Gavroche and Riverside. It might be interesting to see what is charged on the wine list.

Once among the classics of white Bordeaux you are in a strange world, and one which has seldom been explored by the white man, at any rate from England. Château Talbot's Caillou Blanc 1982 has a perfectly pleasant, pebbly taste but a horrible, vaguely biological smell. Many people apparently love it. Corney and Barrow's Château Carbonnieux 1982 is plainly a superior dry white wine, and the same is true of Haynes Hanson's Château Malartic-Lagravière (Graves). Corney and Barrow's Domaine de Chevalier struck me as rather a lot to pay for the taste of high-class cork. But it is when one comes to the last bottle, a Château Laville–Haut-Brion 1980, that one begins to rub one's eyes, or nose, or anything else available. The smell is appalling, the taste gravelly and thin, with a long, slightly metallic after-taste which might remind one of sucking on a dirty tin.

Then I remembered having tasted two examples of this wine – the 1982 and the 1966 – at the Académie du Vin banquet in Paris, and it all came back to me. The 1982 was quite disgusting, the 1966 memorably delicious and unusual. It is a very strange wine, this Laville–Haut-Brion, which completely changes its character after five or six years in the bottle, when the Sémillon comes out on top of the Sauvignon and from tasting like a particularly thin and gravelly Graves it suddenly starts tasting like a de-sugared Sauternes. If one drinks it too early, one is simply throwing money away.

However, these instructions are not written on the bottle, and I honestly feel that more expensive dry white Bordeaux are best left to the experts. At the other end of the market, as I say, there is some good, cheap slurping to be done.

Wines of the Rhône

Throughout most of recorded history the best red wines from the Rhône Valley have generally been thought superior even to Bordeaux. In fact it was only in the eighteenth century that Bordeaux wine-makers began to take themselves seriously at all – until then their wine was treated as a vin de l'année and drunk as soon as people could get their hands on it. As late as the turn of the last century, Hermitage – the richest and fullest of them all, which has been grown in the same place for 2,000 years – was discussed as the equal of Château Lafite.

Hermitage fell from public esteem partly because its production is so tiny – the total area covers only 304 acres of rough and steep terrain – and partly because Bordeaux, being on the Atlantic Coast, was so much more accessible to the international wine trade. Another reason was that the best Hermitage reaches its peak only after twenty years, which is longer than many people were prepared to wait, and a final reason was that the fashion changed – possibly as a result of the three considerations above – towards the thinner, more refined Cabernet Sauvignon of the Médoc and away from the meatiness of the Syrah grape.

Suddenly, wine-drinkers are beginning to take the wines of the Rhône very seriously indeed. They are discovering virtues in the Syrah and Grenache grapes which they had quite forgotten about. Wines of the Rhône Valley have quite simply come to represent the best buy from France.

Various explanations may be put forward for this. Since the insane prices paid for the 1982 premiers crus in Bordeaux nobody in Europe reckons to drink them, although some people have been buying them – I think unwisely – as an investment. The wines of Burgundy have been pricing themselves out of any European market for a long time, as well as having suffered a run of poor vintages in 1974, 1975, 1977, 1980 and 1981. When the growers of the Southern Rhône – most particularly in Château-neuf-du-Pape – tried following Burgundy up the price spiral in the early 1970s, nobody bought their wine, which quite simply accumulated in their cellars until they climbed down and reduced their prices. This resulted in a great flood of mature Châteauneuf-du-Pape on the market, including the miraculous 1967 vintage (after 1961 and possibly 1978, the best in living memory).

But the most amiable explanation is that through economic circumstances, these highly intelligent Europeans have rediscovered one of the great wine-producing areas of France. Even now, the best red wines from Hermitage and best whites from the almost unknown appellations of Condrieu and Château Grillet can compare, after twenty years and five years respectively, with the very best from Châteaux Latour and Margaux or Corton-Charlemagne and Le Montrachet – at half the price in the case of the whites, a quarter in the case of the reds.

At the very north of the Rhône area, the vineyards of Côte Rôtie or 'Scorched Slope', although tiny in area – only 178 acres in 1973, increased to 252 acres last year – were once judged the equal of Hermitage. It was called the Queen of the Rhône, against Hermitage which was thought to be the King. Both are made chiefly from the Syrah grape, but on the Côte Rôtie this was traditionally blended with anything up to 20 per cent of Viognier, the noble white grape which grows only in the Northern Rhône, and then with the greatest difficulty. In recent years, unfortunately, various troubles have afflicted the Côte Rôtie: nobody wants to work the steep, slatey terraces, workers have drifted away and growers have been tempted into overproduction, replacing the difficult Viognier grape or dropping it entirely.

But a few growers still manage to produce the original, magnificent wine which, at its best, is more delicate and feminine than either Hermitage or the best Châteauneuf – notably E. Guigal, at his two properties, La Mouline on the Côte Blonde and La Landonne, on the Côte Brune, and Georges Jasmin, whose wines are slightly less long-lived than either of these, but still retain the authentic Viognier touch.

Just down the Rhône from the Côte Rôtie are the two best white wines of the Rhône and, I would say, of the world – Condrieu and Château Grillet. Both are made exclusively from the Viognier grape which in old age sometimes reverts to the buttery nose and honeyed, cigar-like flintiness of the best old Chardonnay, but at its peak has a wonderful subtle, delicately balanced fruit which I have never found in any other grape. Hugh Johnson swears that these wines should be drunk young, but once, at the Castle Hotel in Taunton, Somerset, we opened three bottles of a Château Grillet 1961. One was on its last legs, the other distinctly fading, but the third was quite simply the best dry white wine I have ever drunk.

Château Grillet is the smallest appellation in France, extending to less than 7½ acres with only one grower and producing about 75 hectoliters a year. Condrieu, with 35 acres and twelve main growers, produces about 310 hectoliters a year. These very rare wines are not at all cheap by the standards of the Rhône because the French fall over themselves to buy them. But only the French have heard of them and they, poor lambs, are not quite so rich as some of us, and if you are lucky enough to find some, you will pay only about half the price of a grand cru white Burgundy. The best grower I have discovered in Condrieu is called Georges Vernay, but Paul Multier and Pierre Dumazet are said to be as good, and they all take enormous trouble to produce the best wine from this very fragile grape. I have yet to drink a glass of either, from any vintage, which was anything but excellent, but they say the 1975 Château Grillet and 1977 Condrieu are at least as good.

Next appellation as one travels south down the Rhône is St Joseph, a poor man's Côte Rôtie. This was granted appellation status only in 1956 and is the lightest of the Northern Rhône reds made predominantly from the Syrah grape. It should be drunk comparatively young and has its admirers. Hugh Johnson and many others back Paul Jaboulet's St Joseph Le Grand Pompée as the best and this is the one I keep trying, but I have yet to find a bottle which was worth being excited about and several I tried were really quite nasty. A better and rather cheaper light Syrah has just been introduced in the Coteaux du Tricastin, Southern Rhône, at the Domaine de la Tour d'Elyssas. I have decided to waste no more time on St Joseph, which also produces an indifferent white made from the Marsanne and Roussanne grapes.

South of St Joseph, and approaching the magnificent sloping cliffs of Hermitage, we must first pass through the village of Crozes-Hermitage which again produces respectable enough wines from the Syrah, but they are a very poor relation of the true Hermitage. Hermitage is the final consummation of the Syrah grape, a great blockbuster of a wine which is just coming into its own after fifteen years in bottle – if you shake it about a bit – but really needs twenty or twenty-five years before you can appreciate the enormous complexity of it. The best I have ever drunk was a 1961 Hermitage La Chapelle from Jaboulet, a branded wine, but they say the 1978 will be as good in fifteen years' time. I have a couple of cases of this in the back of my cellar. The other top growers are Messrs J.-L. Chave, H. Sorrel, J.-L. Grippat and M. Chapoutier, but once again there is no bad wine made in Hermitage.

Parcels of old wine sometimes come up for auction in London. They are one of the great wine experiences available at about a quarter the cost of equivalent clarets. Very good vintages are 1961 (brilliant), 1962, 1964, 1966, 1967, 1969, 1970, 1971, 1972 (excellent, but needs keeping until 1990), 1976, 1978 (brilliant, but keep until the twenty-first century), 1979, 1982 and 1983, said to be the best since 1978. To get some idea of what these wines can taste like, buy an off-vintage like 1977 and open it seven hours before drinking at a few degrees above room temperature.

South of Hermitage one comes to Cornas. Hugh Johnson writes it off as Hermitage's country cousin – all mud and gross, peasant smells. 'Another dark Syrah which only becomes a drink for fastidious palates after many years in bottle', he writes. Well, the worst year in the Northern Rhône is generally reckoned to have been 1975. If Johnson will try a 1975 Cornas from Auguste Clape (generally agreed to be the best grower) I think he will find it puts all his St Joseph Grand Pompée to shame. The other interesting thing about this thick, black-to-purple, intensely concentrated wine is that they say it is the only grape product which can be drunk with Roquefort cheese.

Just south of Cornas is the village of St Péray which makes a heavy rather thick sparkling wine by the champagne method. Personally, I do not find it to my taste. After Valence one is in the Southern Rhône or Côte du Rhône proper, making vast quantities of high-quality table wine whose exports have now overtaken those of Burgundy and Beaujolais. The best red wine unquestionably comes from the huge Châteauneuf-du-Pape area. Many grape varieties are used, predominantly Grenache, and it has long been fashionable to sneer at Châteauneuf as being strong, thick and facile. But there are half a dozen producers whose wine, after ten years or so in the bottle, can undeniably reckon to be numbered among the truly great wines of France: the Domaines du Vieux Télégraphe, Beaucastel and Mont-Redon, Châteaux Fortia and La Nerte, Jaboulet's Les Cèdres, Brunel's Les Cailloux and even Arnaud's Les Silex. The trouble with all these heavy Rhône wines is that unlike young clarets or even five-year-old Burgundies, they taste quite nasty if drunk too young.

The Rhône is an area which produces at least four of the best eight or ten wines of France. When the prices of more famous areas are running amok, wine-lovers ignore it at their peril.

Champagne

On visits to a number of champagne houses this year, enjoying the magnificent hospitality for which the area is famous, I found myself torn between feelings of national shame that we were not doing better and considerable pride that we continue to do so well. Britain is yet again the world's greatest consumer of champagne outside France. Who drinks it all? On a ferry crossing last summer I saw four long-distance lorry drivers, whose accents proclaimed they came from somewhere north of the Trent, get through three bottles of Mumm's Cordon Rouge. In Channel Four's soap opera, 'Brookside', about lower-middle-class life on the Mersey, one observes that they seem to open bottles of champagne at the slightest excuse. I would not be at all surprised to learn that the greater part of our huge total is poured down the throats of exulting workers. I wonder if they pay any attention to the labels.

It scarcely matters either way. The strict standards imposed by the area's own governing body, the Comité Interprofessionel du Vin de Champagne, ensures that there is practically no such thing as a bad bottle of champagne. However, there are bad ways of keeping it. One of them is to keep it standing up on a shelf, and anybody who buys champagne from the off-licence on the corner, or even from a supermarket, rather than from a respectable wine merchant, is risking a drink which has lost all its fruit and most of its taste.

Another way to spoil champagne is to keep it in the fridge too long, and anyone who asks for champagne in a restaurant risks a white-wine-and-soda experience which, although less unpleasant than the sour stuff which has been left standing in a heated shop for many weeks, is still a great waste of money – particularly at restaurant prices.

Champagne

Although, as I say, there is practically no such thing as a bad bottle of champagne out of Reims or Epernay, there are bad times of day to drink it, and the worst is almost certainly four o'clock in the afternoon, after a Society wedding when guests have queued for half an hour to risk every sort of infection by kissing the bride. Goodness knows how the idea ever arose that it was a good idea to be married at two o'clock in the afternoon, but I suspect it was decided by the meanness of brides' parents through the ages, and their determination not to feed their guests. Merciful common sense seems to be breaking through in the new trend for 12 o'clock weddings. Food is really not very expensive to provide unless you go to a fashionable caterer. The best thing is not to go to a fashionable caterer but to a commercial one – those who advertise 'Bar-mitzvahs a speciality' are usually the best – tell him exactly what you want and insist on ordering the champagne yourself. Insist also on thin goblets rather than the ghastly saucer-shaped jelly bowls which English caterers favour. Thin goblets are sensible for many reasons, not least of which is that those who do not really like champagne can hold one glass all afternoon without spilling it. The jelly bowls have nothing to recommend them except that they make you sneeze. Some people enjoy sneezing very much indeed.

When everything else has been decided there still remains the matter of what champagne to serve. My own observation is that guests generally respond more positively to Bollinger than to Moët and Chandon, although Moët is a highly respectable wine and, unless it has been abominably maltreated, quite justifies its position as the biggest-selling champagne in Britain. About Lanson, another front-runner, I am not so sure, although its inexpensive rosé is almost universally acceptable. But the preference for Bollinger which I have observed among guests who are given several champagnes to taste and asked to choose between them leads me to various conclusions.

There are just three grape varieties in champagne – Chardonnay (the grape of white Burgundy), Pinot Noir (the grape of red Burgundy) and Pinot Meunier (another red grape, generally thought of as a bit of a space-filler). Bollinger is noted for its high proportion of Pinot Noir, rising to 100 per cent of Pinot Noir in its magnificent de luxe range called Vieilles Vignes. If I am right then the English, without knowing it, generally prefer the heavier Pinot

Noir taste to the fizzy Chablis style of Chardonnay and the blancs de blanc. A cheaper version of the Bollinger style is available from the neighbouring property of Château d'Ay, marketed as Ayala, which was immensely popular with the Edwardians but has now fallen from fashion, possibly because the name has down-market associations.

But Ayala should really not be confused with Coca-Cola – it is a great wine, sadly unknown today, as is another grande marque champagne, Billecart-Salmon, exclusively imported by Mr Mark Savage of Windrush Wines.

My theory that the English prefer the Pinot Noir taste in champagne might explain why Taittinger, which is a best-seller in America, has never really taken off here. In the luxury class, the Americans have always gone for Louis Roederer's Cristal, while the English remain faithful to Krug, which has a surprisingly high percentage of Pinot Meunier. Claude Taittinger, the present head of the firm, assured me that he had never particularly tried to cultivate the English market, but it is noticeable that even really well-made champagne like Pommery, which is also notable for its strong Chardonnay element, has never really hit the English market.

Neither Roederer nor Laurent-Perrier, which has seen a spectacular growth since the war under M. Bernard de Nonancourt, has made Taittinger's mistake of investing huge sums in automatic *remuage* machines. Biochemical advances may soon make the whole *remuage* process unnecessary. I suspect that Taittinger will soon find himself hit hard by improvements in the Californian product. But Britain remains a steady market for all the best champagne houses, and those of them which are still in private ownership seem to retain a special affection for Britain: Christian de Billy's Pol Roger; Christian Bizot's Bollinger; Jean-Claude Rouzaud's Louis Roederer; Bernard de Nonancourt's Laurent-Perrier. Perhaps my favourite of all is Krug's Grande Cuvée, but that is now too murderously expensive for most people. But I feel we have a patriotic duty to drink as much as we can.

Whilst on a visit to the Pommery and Greno establishment in Reims, I was shown their rosé or pink champagne. I had never tasted it before. It is a magnificent wine, much fuller and more robust than a normal champagne.

It is a curious thing that a number of leading wine merchants in this country do not stock pink champagne at all, including the Wine Society, Harvey's and Avery's of Bristol, Corney and Barrow... When I spoke to Corney and Barrow about this, they said they were thinking of trying the Laurent-Perrier rosé. This is the most popular pink at present – in fact it is a pink-orange colour, and quite delicious even if it lacks the weight of the Pommery.

Laurent-Perrier are extending their rosé operation and Krug itself, after 140 years in the business, has just launched a rosé. It is perfectly delicious – very pale, just like a vintage white brut, but premier. Moët and Chandon have launched an excellent 1978 rosé which beats, at any rate in my humble opinion, their ordinary 1978 vintage brut. My own guess is that we are just about to enter an age of pink champagne. Nothing will ever persuade the French that we don't like their brut, and there is something agreeably Barbara Cartlandish, suitable for the new romantic era, about returning to this great Edwardian favourite. Perhaps it cannot compare, in delicacy or subtlety, to the very best white champagne, but how many of us ever drink the very best? In the middle price ranges it is usually as good as or better than its white equivalents, and much more festive to look at. But if people are determined to stick to ordinary white champagne, despite being nauseated as often as not by its sharpness and fizziness, I do earnestly advise them to try some extra sec or sec rather than brut and insist on the crémant or half-sparkling version of their favourite champagne, which is much less gaseous.

The Loire

On a recent visit to the Loire, I found myself time and again raving about certain wines I found in Sancerre and the neighbouring, smaller appellation of Ménétou-Salon. All my life I had been proclaiming that the wines of the Loire, with very few exceptions indeed, are a snare and a delusion. They are sharp and thin and generally rather nasty, whatever one may think of them when served in one of the excellent restaurants of Tours or Nantes or Bourges. I resolved to track them down and try them again in England before writing about them.

First a run-through of the main Loire wines, starting from the east. From the south and west of Nantes comes all the astringent white Muscadet which is at present flooding supermarkets and chainstores in Britain. It is possible to find reasonably good Muscadet from the Sèvre and Maine area, but very difficult in this country. I have the impression that the French drink all the best stuff. Muscadet enjoys a good reputation largely on the memory of good examples found in France, and people in England pretend to enjoy it more than they do because it is so cheap. They say it goes particularly well with fish, and this may be true of raw shellfish, but everything goes particularly well with ordinary white fish. The only way to be sure of getting a good Muscadet is to go to an expensive wine merchant, but I would not really recommend it cxccpt, as I say, with raw shellfish.

After Nantes, the Anjou–Saumur region produces, in my experience, absolutely nothing but filth. This is the area of the Chenin Blanc grape which the South Africans, oddly enough, do wonderful things with. In France it becomes a horrible sweet and sour taste which a few people relish, but not many. It is at its most horrible, by my reckoning, in the expensive 'dessert' wines of the

Coteaux du Layon – Quarts de Chaume (said to taste of quinces), Bonnezeaux and Moulin Touchais. It is easy to find examples of their wines which are fifty, sixty, seventy, even eighty years old but they are no less disgusting than yesterday's. Also to be avoided from this area are the white wines of Saumur, whether flat or fizzy, and anything pink with the word 'Anjou' on its label.

Next, around Tours, there are fewer pitfalls, although I tend to avoid anything from Vouvray. They say that Vouvray has produced and still produces in tiny areas some of the best and grandest sweet wine in the world, but I have never tasted it. As found in English shops, it is a characterless, medium sweet wine of some considerable horror. The fizzy variety is even worse.

But Touraine also produces some perfectly decent, if only quite exciting, red wines, which visitors to the area fall upon with cries of wonder: Bourgueil and St-Nicolas de Bourgueil, which I have written about before, are the best. I think I drank a good Chinon about twelve years ago – it is made from the same grape as Bourgueil, the Cabernet Franc – but my last five attempts have been failures, so now I have given up. People say it reminds them of violets and wild strawberries, but I feel they must be mad.

After Touraine, and skirting Orléans, whose wine is not worth writing about, one hits Sancerre and Ménétou-Salon, the areas of which I treat. To the West again, just across the Loire, lie the famous vineyards of Pouilly Fumé, which by my reckoning have become altogether too famous for their own good. I have drunk some wonderful Pouilly Fumés in my time, but none recently. Practically every restaurant of any pretension in Britain has it on its wine list, and it is nearly always thin, sour and lifeless. Obviously there are some good examples around, but no British wine merchant has been able to show me one on his current list, and I would advise people to buy examples of this wine only on the recommendation of a trusted friend.

So let us go back across the river to Sancerre and its neighbouring Ménétou-Salon. Their white wines are almost indistinguishable, both made from Sauvignon Blanc, the same grape as is used in white Bordeaux, but something wonderful seems to have happened in the area since they introduced cold fermentation for these white wines. One is generally safer with a Ménétou-Salon than a Sancerre, since less second-rate wine is produced by the smaller, less famous region. But both, at their best, are absolutely magnificent, with a knock-out bouquet of flowers and newly-cut grass, masses of fruit and one of the liveliest, cleanest tastes I have yet discovered.

To those who have never tried red Sancerre – I confess I was among their number until recently – I should explain that it is totally unlike any other red wine they are likely to have tasted, although Hugh Johnson compares its faintly watery style to German Spätburgunder, which I have always found disgusting. It has long been more popular in France than in Britain – Parisians lap it up. On first discovering it I had a Chapman's Homer experience. Subsequent quaffing confirms that it is an ideal drink for summer lunchtime – light, elegant and fruity with a faint aroma of rosehips. One can drink it by the bottle without difficulty, still marvelling at its powers of refreshment.

Normally I would sympathise with those who say that wine has no business to have a faint aroma of rosehips, and can only reply that on this occasion it works. Some may not like it, even when drunk slightly chilled out of doors, but some people are impossible to please. Sancerre rouge is pale in colour and made from the Pinot Noir grape, sharing the nose you sometimes find in old Volnay, red Meursault and Montagny. But there the resemblance to Burgundy ends.

---

101 Alsatians

My reason for choosing to devote almost an entire section to the wines of Alsace is that the shops are still full of the magnificent 1983 vintage – certainly as good as the fabled 1976s, arguably better than any since 1959. So long as these beautiful wines are available, English wine-drinkers would be mad not to investigate them, since we may have to wait many years for anything as good.

Wines from Alsace are predominantly white, with a few boring rosés and some bad red Pinot Noirs – that is to say, I have never tasted a good Alsatian red, although others claim to have done so. I will confine myself to the 1983 whites, which, as I say, are stupendous, and still easily available. Alsatian whites divide into Edelzwicker wines, which are usually branded blends, and single-grape varietals made from the six main Alsatian grapes. These are Sylvaner, usually the cheapest and lightest, sometimes a little acid and with the slightest touch of effervescence; Pinot Blanc (also called Klevner), which has less acid, a fresh, light, dry wine which often represents good value for money; Muscat, producing a dry, grapey, surprisingly fragrant wine from the same grape which produces luscious dessert wines in the South; the Tokay d'Alsace, also called Pinot Gris, capable of a deeper, smokier, more spicy taste than the first two; Riesling, producing a drier, fresher wine than its German equivalent, with no hint of residual sugar; and finally the grape for which Alsace is most famous outside France, the Gewürztraminer, which is the spiciest and most characteristic of them all, with a taste which has sometimes been compared to the smell of fresh sheep's droppings. Gewürztraminer, which is my favourite of Alsace varietals, is probably the only wine (apart from champagne) which goes well with such strongly flavoured food as smoked salmon, grilled sardines or herrings, and curries.

All the wines I have mentioned present themselves as dry, but the Riesling, Tokay and Gewürztraminer grapes also lend themselves in certain years to deeper, more concentrated and sweeter versions called vendange tardive, which is the equivalent of the German Auslese, and sélection de grains nobles, which is the equivalent of Beerenauslese. At the time of writing, few of these sweeter, nobler 1983s have been released, but they promise to be block-busters when they are.

In the great question of which Riesling, which Gewürztraminer or Muscat to buy, the simplest advice is to go for one of the big négociants or growers. Hugel has never let me down, but he is also the most expensive. The other names one sees quite often are, in my own descending order of preference, Dopff, Schmidt, Trimbach and Laugel, but all are good and all are cheaper than Hugel.

But if one is going to take these Alsatian wines seriously, one should shop around, whether one is interested in bargains or in particular excellence. Recently, Sainsbury's was selling a perfectly adequate Gewürz on their own label – perhaps it was sweeter than it should have been, but I would choose it in preference to a sparkling Vouvray for a wedding on any day of the week. Many of the smaller wine merchants have their own grocer or négociant in Alsace, having searched him out for themselves, and then sell the whole range of his wines. Windrush Wines, a highly discriminating importer, has settled on Zind-Humbrecht, well known in Alsace if not yet in this country. Robin Yapp, of Yapp Brothers, has fixed on a vigneron called Charles Schleret and swears by his individual genius. Young Nicholas Davies, of the Hungerford Wine Company, has gone nap on a fellow called Gisselbrecht in Dambach-La-Ville, although he also stocks Hugel for those who can't pronounce the other one. Most expensive of all, O. W. Loeb have taken on the agency for Faller Frères.

I am not sure that the more expensive Alsatians are really colossal value for money, but they are exceptionally pleasant wines. Both the Gewürz and the dry Muscat provide taste sensations which are peculiar to themselves, and it would be a shame to miss the opportunity of exploring them while the glorious 1983 vintage is still around.

Little-known Wines of France

Of all wine bores, some of the worst are those who have just come back from a holiday in France and discovered an exquisite new wine which costs practically nothing and is known about in only a few villages around where it is produced. They can seldom remember its name accurately but they assure you that for six or seven francs a bottle it knocks Château Lafite (if red) or Montrachet (if white) for six.

Unless they are referring to some mass-produced branded wine which they bought at the groceries, it is usually possible for anyone with a wine library to trace the wine they are talking about by reference to the village or town where they found it. If, like me, you collect wine catalogues from small and obscure wine importers all over the country, it is sometimes possible even to track down a bottle. The result is always disappointing.

One excuse which is often advanced is that this exquisite little wine is one which cannot travel. In former times, when wine was transported by horses and oxen, slurping around in dirty wooden casks, it was certainly true that some wines suffered in transit, especially whites and light reds which relied on their freshness. Nowadays there is no such excuse. No wine yet invented could fail to survive the short journey from any part of France to any part of Britain in bottle. The real explanation is that British wine-drinkers commonly drink less good French wine in France than they do in England, where price differences are less noticeable. When, on a sunny day and with a good meal, they find a reasonably good wine (which they have chosen as the cheapest on the wine list at their restaurant) they become violently over-excited. Back in England, and paying at least £2.50 a bottle for their brilliant discovery – probably nearer £3.50 – they begin to see things in perspective.

Little-known Wines of France

The sad truth is that the best wines in France come from the five greatest wine-producing areas of Bordeaux, Burgundy, Beaujolais, the Rhône, Champagne and Alsace. These wines are also the most expensive – the French aren't fools – and no amount of wishful thinking can alter this melancholy fact. There are perfectly good wines to be found in some of the lesser wine-producing areas – the Loire, the Dordogne, Languedoc-Roussillon in the Midi, Provence, even Savoie in the Alps, Vichy in the middle of France and around Armagnac in the Southwest – but as soon as these wines begin to approach excellence, their prices rise steeply. The French, as I say, are not fools, and they are just as greedy and as mean as superior English folk in search of a bargain.

The most common noise one hears is from English folk with small properties in the Dordogne or Lot who come back extolling the wines of Bergerac or (in the case of meaner or poorer travellers) Gaillac. Bergerac produces some perfectly decent wines, well worth drinking in France at eleven or twelve francs the bottle. The reds are light, claret-style drinks and some of the whites – especially one called Rosetta, which is so mild as to be almost tasteless – slip down very easily. But in England, where they can cost around £3.50 a bottle, they simply do not compare in their price range with wines of similar quality from Spain. Again the wines of Gaillac, which can cost as little as seven or eight francs a bottle in France, are actually quite inferior wines, with the exception of a few perlé (slightly sparkling) whites which compare favourably with the same sort of stuff which comes flooding in from Portugal.

But, as I say, there are some magnificent wines to be found in the minor wine-producing areas, so long as one can separate one's urge towards new experiences from one's bargain-hunting urges. People returning from Provence and the Côte d'Azur often sing about the rosés and whites they have found in St Tropez or from the Domaines d'Ott or Bellet, but these wines are hideously overpriced even in France. The only wine produced in Provence which is worth bringing back to England is called Bandol – a beautiful, swarthy, scorched-earth red which improves with keeping.

Further north, in the southern reaches of the Rhône, I persist in believing that the best rosé in the world comes from Tavel, although I have heard the same claim made for a wine called

Marsannay from near Dijon in the very north of Burgundy, and even for Tavel's next-door neighbour and poor relation, Lirac, which is certainly rather cheaper. If one forgets the two great names of the Rhône – Hermitage and Châteauneuf-du-Pape – one finds some very pleasant surprises in the same line of business labelled Cornas Gigondas and even Saint Joseph.

The Rhône also produces the best sweet Muscat in the world, called Beaumes de Venise, but this is beginning to be so famous that I fear we will not be able to afford it much longer. One can root around the Midi–Languedoc for other Muscats – from Rivesaltes, Frontignan and Mireval – but they are not nearly so good. In fact nothing worth getting excited about comes out of the huge Languedoc region. One or two red Corbières are quite good, but they are so hard to find, and vary so much from year to year, that it is best to avoid the label altogether. The same is true of Roussillon reds to the south, although I once found a startlingly good old one in Collioure, but now I have forgotten the name...

Minervois is probably the most reliable of the Languedoc reds. The best I have found is a branded co-operative called Clos des Papes, which is not exported. There is also a small, up-and-coming VDQS area called Saint Chinian which is worth trying if you find a bottle. The Midi produces some reasonable 'green wine' at Roussillon and a bogus champagne called Blanquette de Limoux of which Christopher's of Chelsea sell the best examples at less than half the price of champagne.

But the most exciting and varied of the minor wine areas of France is undoubtedly the Loire. This produces such a huge variety of wine, ranging from the viciously over-priced with a really nasty taste to some of the most agreeable wines of France, but until one has studied the area in detail, the best advice is to avoid anything which comes from Anjou and try anything from Touraine.

Provence – a Red and a White

The Coteaux d'Aix en Provence Blanc is a perfectly decent wine for serving to young girls at a party. It has no distinction whatever and not even a tremendous amount of taste, but what does distinguish it from other cheap whites is that it has no nasty tastes, either. It is a clean wine which will not turn sour or make the breath smell and screw up the digestive system even if taken in large amounts. Of course if you serve young people a nastier wine they might drink less, but this is by no means always certain and nasty wine often makes them sick.

The Coteaux d'Aix en Provence Rouge, which comes in the same silly Provencal 75cl bottle – I do not know why people down there suppose we will be amused by their idiotic bottle shapes – is an altogether fuller and more satisfying drink experience. Although the young women on my panel were also loud in their approval, I should judge it an acceptable drink for all ages, with more than enough body to see proper, middle-aged wine-drinkers through the spring and summer months. It is pale in colour (my elder son, a musician, described it approvingly as lymph-red) but has the great warm southern Rhône taste which one would expect from a darker wine. Perhaps its appearance would be against it for the winter months, but a wonderful drink for summer.

G E R M A N Y

Great German Wines

With the world's vineyards at their feet, over 70 per cent of wine-drinkers in Britain still choose to drink semi-sweet table wine imported from Germany, usually a blend of Common Market wines with sugar added, in preference to anything else. In so far as the British have a national taste for wine, it would appear that better-grade Liebfraumilch just about fills the ticket. We like our wine sweetish with a touch of acid to give it bounce, white and low in alcohol. Sichel's Blue Nun Liebfraumilch and Langenbach's Crown of Crowns are our idea of very heaven, but we happily drink much nastier stuff if the price is right.

Perhaps because of this passion for filth on the part of the hoi polloi, the better estate-bottled German wines are scarcely given a chance. Discriminating wine-drinkers avoid Germany altogether, except for a small handful of enthusiasts. We tend to buy our Rieslings and Gewürztraminers from Alsace, in France, although they are generally more expensive, and even go to Alsace for their equivalent of the Auslese quality, called vendange tardive, which is often vastly more expensive and seldom as good.

This may be a good moment to take an interest in German wines, since 1983 was by general agreement a brilliantly good year on the Rhine and Nahe, while on the Mosel it was the best since the great classic year of 1976. It was while investigating the 1983 vintage – the Southwold firm of Adnams has a large choice of 1983s for laying down and drinking now – that I discovered stocks of the 1976 wine still lying around unsold in London wine merchants at what seem to me spectacularly low prices. I suspect there are two reasons for this. The first is a comparative lack of demand, as explained above. The second is that wine lying in cellars is not subject to all the inflationary pressures which bear upon the unfortunate wine producer and importer, especially in the light of our own sinking currency. The result of these two considerations is that the wines of 1976 – a classic year, now in most cases at its peak – are around the same price as those for 1983, which was a brilliant year for Spätlesen, rapidly becoming the most popular of the three main German grades of wine, although not producing large quantities of the richer, sweeter and more expensive Auslesen.

Perhaps I should briefly explain how German wines are graded. First, the sheep are separated from the goats. Anything called Tafelwein or simply marked Qualitätswein without the all-important further description 'mit Prädikat' has had sugar added, and should be avoided by serious wine-drinkers. The description Qualitätswein mit Prädikat will sometimes be abbreviated to QmP. This is not the same as QbA, which should be avoided. I am not really prepared to say what QbA stands for, in case I am accused of pulling people's legs. Oh, all right. It stands for Qualitätswein bestimmter Anbaugebiete. Some 95 per cent of German wine is classified in that way, which shows how seriously they take it all. It means that the wine comes from a specified region, but in plain English it means it is pretty good rubbish.

'Mit Prädikat' means 'with distinction', and there are six grades of distinction available. They are: Kabinett, Spätlese, Auslese, Beerenauslese, Eiswein, Trochenbeerenauslese. Only the first three need be of interest to the English wine-drinker, since the last three are so rare, so expensive and so highly prized by the Germans themselves that it seems foolish as well as cruel to join the competition for them. The Germans are much richer than we are, in any case. But sometimes they will serve you a glass, and then it is as well to make the appropriate noises.

The grades are decided with typical German thoroughness by an elaborate system of weighing the must or newly-pressed juice and estimating the potential alcohol content (that is to say, what its alcoholic strength would be if it were allowed to ferment into a dry wine). The Germans have decided that these are what determine the wine's ultimate quality, and they certainly determine its concentration of flavour. A rough and not entirely accurate guide for the layman might suggest that generally speaking the further down the list you move the higher the natural sugar content and so

Great German Wines

the sweeter the wine. This is not entirely true, as I have suggested, since there are some exceptions and measurement of sweetness alone does not take into account such factors as acid level and what might be called the botrytis factor. Botrytis is not a disease but a process of evaporation in hot autumns which shrivels the grape, concentrates the juice and adds a particular taste of its own, familiar to all dessert wine-lovers. But to say that the higher the grade the sweeter the wine is probably true enough to be getting on with.

So let us start with the Kabinett. These are usually the driest and least expensive of the unsugared German wines, but they are still too sweet to drink with a meal, by my reckoning. They and the Spätlesen make excellent aperitifs, in the modern fashion for avoiding gin, sherry and all the grosser pre-prandial drinks, or they can be drunk as a healthier night-cap than whisky after a long evening of smoking and talking. They are also the only wines I have discovered which go well with pot, having a soothing and fragrant influence.

Kabinett wines are best drunk young, and 1983 produced some really excellent examples. The best ones I found from the huge stocks held by the House of Hallgarten were an excellently fruity Mainzer Domherr from the Rheinhessen and a Wiltinger Scharzberg, from the Saar, at the other end of the Riesling Kabinett spectrum being less sweet, with slightly more acid, and miraculously refreshing without any great weight of fruit.

Spätlesen come a little sweeter and more concentrated. The best 1983 I tasted was a Mosel wine, the Bernkasteler Craben from Deinhard, available from Adnams. It is a beautiful wine, with acid and fruit perfectly in balance, and would make a more elegant and less obvious aperitif than most champagnes at that price. Much cheaper and nearly as good was Hallgarten's St Johanner Ablei Spätlese from the Rheinhessen, an amazingly rich wine.

Now we come to the Auslesen, which need to be kept much longer. The 1976 Auslesen are now drinking beautifully – too sweet, I would judge, for anything except the end of the meal, although the Germans do not agree. If only people still ate savoury courses, they would go very well with chicken livers wrapped in bacon, mushrooms on toast, Welsh rarebit and things like that.

Hallgarten knocked me sideways with the excellence of his 1976

Auslesen. Large stocks are also held by O.W. Loeb but I have not tasted them, and I have an uneasy feeling one may be paying a little extra for that address. Of Peter Hallgarten's collection, I thought the best value for money was not from the Riesling grape but from one of the new crossings – a Dienheimer Siliusbrunnen Faberrebe Auslese 1976. This was a really beautiful sweet and fruity wine, with a slightly waterish ending. Best of the lot was a 1976 Wiltinger Kupp Riesling Auslese, with its delicious honeyed concentration – the nearest most of us will get to the last three categories of German wines.

Those who wish to learn more on the subject should buy a copy of Ian Jamieson's *German Wines* in Mitchell Beazley's brilliant series of pocket guides which includes Hugh Johnson's *Pocket Wine Book*.

ITALY

Vino Very Tasty

1984 was bad for many French wine-growers, but in Italy it seems to have been a total disaster. The wine trade tends to shy away from such expressions, especially, of course, the Italian specialists, since they will eventually have to try to sell the stuff. But every independent source of information points to 1984 being remembered as a great wash-out in Italy – especially in the vineyards north of Rome where all the best Italian reds are to be found. In Florence, it rained every day from mid-August until 11 October while the grapes should have been ripening. On 8 October, traditionally a time for the harvest or vendemmia to be in full swing, the level of the River Arno rose three metres, as water poured out of the soggy vineyards. Further north, in the excellent vineyards of Friuli-Venezia-Giulia where wine-makers are beginning to take their job seriously, the story was much the same.

The result of all this is that practically no Chianti will appear, or any other wine bearing a DOC (Denominazione di Origine Controllata) label for the year. They will all be declassified as table wine (vino di tavola) so nobody will be able to buy any of the wines mentioned here unless the Italians release large stocks of 1983's excellent and abundant vintage. If they do – and this is the silver lining – English wine-drinkers will at last have an opportunity to drink these beautiful, thick, concentrated wines as they should be drunk, rather than as the Italians want us to drink them.

If the Italians have a fault – and, goodness knows, they *do* – it is to push out their wine as soon as it has finished bubbling and giving off poisonous gases. To do them justice, that is how they like to drink it themselves. Until recently, they have been reluctant to take wine seriously at all, regarding it rather as the Irish regard potatoes: an inevitable but not very interesting accompaniment to every meal. They are the biggest producers of wine in the world, and also the biggest consumers. But whereas their production has been steadily increasing – in 1983 they produced eight billion litres, nearly a quarter of the world's production – their consumption has been shrinking. In 1968 they drank 116 litres of wine a head which, as the figures include small children, teetotallers, nuns and the whole non-drinking community, was quite an impressive figure. By 1981, however, their consumption had fallen to 74 litres a head. Obviously, there was a need to export wine, but as most of their wine was exported for blending into acceptable plonk in France and Germany, and as all the wine-drinking nations of the world (except Britain) are now retreating from plonk, they were left with the only option, terrible in its implications and contrary to the whole Italian wine-growing tradition: they had to improve their wine.

And so they did. 1984, of course, is an exception, and they can return to their traditional habits. It has been said that if you leave an Italian with a butt of rainwater, four mail-bags of mislaid holiday postcards and a hundredweight of banana skins, he will produce twenty cases of vino di tavola within a fortnight. The 1984 harvest will test their ingenuity, and I suspect that the only people to profit will be the grocers who supply them with (illegal) sacks of sugar.

But apart from the few great Italian wines which I will be discussing, and which will certainly not appear from the 1984 harvest, there is a new breed of Italian wines from the north of Italy, made from serious grapes like Cabernet Sauvignon, Merlot, Malbec, even Pinot Nero, as well as Chardonnay and the slightly more traditional Italian white grapes like Pinot Bianco, Pinot Grigio and Tocai. These would be serious and excellent wines if only the wine-makers could be persuaded to keep them for eighteen months in bottle before selling them. Italian wines, I should explain, seem to advance in bottle much, much faster than their French equivalents. I remember a Pinot Nero from the Vinicola Udinese which made a brilliant wine in 1979 – as good as anything from Santenay or Givry in the same year at quarter the price – and which I discovered in, I think, 1982 when the wine merchant concerned was running out of stocks. When I reordered he followed it up with the 1980, which arrived as a hideous,

Vino Very Tasty

chaptalised purple fizz. Within six months, it had settled into something quite drinkable.

Perhaps, as I say, the failure of the 1984 Italian wine harvest will eventually prove a blessing, not only to the English wine-drinker but also to the serious Italian wine-makers of Tuscany and the north of Italy. It is a dreadful shame seeing people quite reasonably refusing to buy wine which they have never heard of, and which tastes disgusting now, when in twelve or eighteen months' time they will have an excellent wine at a bargain price. But the Italian wine trade is its own worst enemy. Where the growers of Rioja in Spain spend £250,000 a year in Britain on generic advertising, the Italians spend practically nothing.

Thirty years ago, Chianti was a staple drink of the English middle classes. Schoolmasters served it at their little dinner parties, nurses served it by candlelight in the fifth-floor Fulham flats they shared with eight other nurses. Now it has been completely overtaken by the Spanish – partly, no doubt, because more people have been going to Spain on their holidays but chiefly, as I maintain, because of the Italian ineptitude at marketing it. Nearly all the DOC Italian reds are extraordinarily cheap for their quality and highly drinkable even when they have been left standing on an off-licence shelf for three months. Try Peter Dominic's Cabernet from the Villa Catezzana at Carmignano.

I know of only two English merchants specialising in Italian wines, although no doubt there are others. The first is in Hampshire, Stonehaven Wines. I have had no dealings with them myself, but they stock wine from many of the best producers and it is a field which is well worth investigating. The other Italian specialist – and the one I use – is the ebullient, resourceful, forty-five-year-old young Colin 'High' Price-Beech of Recount Wines. He has good, slurping Chianti Putto from Amici Grossi, and a highly recommendable white Chardonnay from Eno Friulia. His best wine in the middle range, I thought, was a Pignatelli production from Castell'in Villa – a serious and considerable wine. I have never tasted the most expensive Italian on his list, a huge Barolo from Elvio Cogno at La Morra, although Burton Anderson, our greatest expert on Italian wine, describes Cogno wine as being 'constantly among the best and most sought-after Barolo'.

The very best Italian wine of all is by general consent the Brunello di Montalcino of Biondi Santi which is very rare indeed and likely to cost up to £70 a bottle. I have never tasted it and certainly do not propose to spend £70 on a bottle of anything from these Holy Blonds. But two seriously excellent wines, both handled by Antinori, are imported by Hedges & Butler. Tignanello, everybody's first example of a serious Italian wine, is one of the new claret-style reds made by Antinori in Tuscany, but if it gets any more famous it will not be able to compete with its equivalent price range in Bordeaux. The other is called Sassicaia, made from exclusively Cabernet grapes by the Incisa family at Bolgheri, near Livorno. In a grand tasting of Cabernet wines sponsored by *Decanter* magazine in 1978, this Sassicaia, in Burton Anderson's words, 'swept the field of 34 wines from eleven nations, winning unprecedented perfect scores of 20 from two of five panellists and the unanimous accolade of "the best wine in the entire tasting"'. I hope the French looked sheepish. I feel we owe it to the Italians to try this miraculous wine, if only to convince ourselves of what they can do.

Claret Substitutes from Italy

After the inflated prices asked for 1982 and 1983 clarets, it seemed a good time to find a substitute for these over-priced Bordeaux, so I undertook a trip to the north-east Italian wine-producers of the Tre Venezie, Fruili, Collio and the Alto Adige where for some time now growers have been developing the classic French grapes of Bordeaux – Merlot, Cabernet Sauvignon, Cabernet Franc and Malbec. They are also doing their best with the Pinot Noir grape of Burgundy, but I did not find a single successful example of Italian Pinot Nero this year, so propose to ignore them all and concentrate on undercutting the Bordeaux.

Wine-buyers may feel there is something distinctly odd in the idea of buying Italian wines for laying down. Certainly the Italians have not got used to the idea yet. They are accustomed to gulping down their wines (at any rate outside Piedmont) as soon as they appear, with the result that even the best Venetian restaurants – La Colombo, the Fenice Taverna and my new discovery, Al Giardiretto, a converted fifteenth-century chapel near the Zaccharia – push these serious and excellent wines at you in a sour and stalky state only a few months out of the barrel. The point about buying these Italians to lay down is that they cost less than half of what the equivalent quality would cost from Bordeaux and they mature at about three times the speed. At the end of the day you have a first-class wine, even if the only prestige attaching to them now is the slightly invidious satisfaction of serving good wine more cheaply than anyone else.

In a hard course of tastings, I picked out two Merlots and three Cabernets which seemed to me of outstanding quality. These were all produced for me by Mr Gowan Hall of Talbon Wines (Castello 5025, Venezia, telephone (041)-21588). With the exception of the first, they are none of them ready to drink yet (unless, like the Italians, you enjoy the tastes of tannin, stalk, ink, fruit juice, sherbert, iron and sundry fermentation gases) but most of them will be ready in fifteen months and all will be drinking splendidly in two years.

The first and most immediately drinkable was Livio Felluga's Merlot of 1981, from Fruili. Livio must not be confused with his brother Marco, a more commercial wine-maker who does not achieve the same standards. This Merlot (the grape which gives their distinctive taste to Pomerol and St Emilion wines in Bordeaux) is a seriously decent wine – substantial and round with a full, fat finish. The second Merlot I picked out – Dal Moro's Pramaggiore 1982 – remains a little sharp at the finish, being a year younger, but it has plenty of guts and personality, comes from one of the best wine-makers in the area and will certainly make excellent drinking in nine months' time.

Cabernet is more particularly the grape of the Médoc. The three Cabernets I picked out will all need a little longer, but a 1983 Cabernet Franc de Brazzano, from the Colli Orientali di Friuli, was extraordinarily forward with an excellent nose when drunk from the barrel. It was still showing too much tannin and iron for English tastes, but in eighteen months' time it will certainly be worth trying again. Of the other two, a 1983 Collio Cabernet Franc seemed to be shaping up on the sweet side through all the fizz and gas which surrounded it, while Dal Moro's Pramaggiore 1983 Cabernet seemed to be shaping up on the dry side of perfection, but both were beautifully-made wines which should be worth waiting for.

More Italian Delights

The San Giovese di Romagna 1984 is an extraordinarily fruity product of rather a thin year in the Romagna with a rare and beautiful hare's blood or red garnet colour and a fragrance of freshly cut pine – not the stale, resinated taste of Greek wine but the overpowering smell of pine forests. One could speak of its generous fruit or its chewy back-bite, and there can be no doubt that it provides a very pleasant drink for those with no preconceptions about what wine should taste like. Those who *have* such preconceptions might suspect it had been doctored. I put this to Price-Beech, who swore that cru Moronico (*sic*) was one of the most respectable wines in Romagna, and that it is inconceivable that Tommaso Vallunga, the wine-maker, would do such a thing. I believe him. Its enemies might talk of boiled sweets, but they are the very best boiled sweets and it is certainly a rich drink at the price.

My great discovery is a Barolo called La Brunate 1980 from Poderi Marcarini. This is a seriously excellent wine, which I would call scrumptious. It has a rich, thick, malty taste cut by just the right amount of acid to ensure that it will grow and grow in the bottle. I never knew the Italians could make wine like this. It is a real winner, deserving comparison with any of the world's best wines.

S P A I N

Spanish Wines

Most of the enormous quantity of wine produced in Spain is pretty poor stuff and some of it is horrible. The country is too hot and the natives are too careless in their wine-making. When British wine-drinkers began to realise they could no longer afford even the second-rank wines of France, there was a stampede for red Rioja. Throughout the 1970s, this was the chief tipple at wine and cheese parties in a good cause. Buying was indiscriminate – imports from the Rioja region alone rose ten times during the decade – and some really nasty wine was drunk. Even today you should never buy Riojas from your local grocer unless you happen to know it already. Bad Spanish wine furs the tongue, turns the breath sour, upsets the stomach and produces a murderous hangover. Some of the unwritten tragedies of the period are surely to be found among those hopeful and idealistic nurses and secretaries who lost their virginity with a foul taste in their mouths, a bad tummy-ache and incipient headache to lovers whose breath stank of sewage.

Nowadays it is quite easy to find seriously excellent wine from Spain at half or even quarter the price of its French equivalent. Here I will mention only two suppliers, partly because I believe them to be the best in the field and partly because, as they are direct importers, their wines are liable to be considerably cheaper. But many of the wines I mention may be found elsewhere at slightly higher prices. The important thing, I would say, is to buy from a wine merchant rather than a grocery or department store, unless the department store – like Sainsbury's and Marks and Spencer's – makes a big effort with its wines.

First of the better Riojas to arrive and create an impression was the Marqués de Riscal SA, from the Rioja Alavesas. This comes in a beautiful label, rather like Pichon Longueville Baron, and covered with gold wire, like something on a Christmas tree. It is a light, dry, distinctly elegant wine, which remains a favourite among the less adventurous wine-drinkers in this country. It is available from Laymont and Shaw, of The Old Chapel, Millpool, Truro, Cornwall TR1 1EX (0872-70545).

Riscal's great rival for the English market was always another marquess, the Marqués de Murrieta, whose famous bodega in the Rioja Alta makes the superb red Castillo Ygay. Spaniards prefer the fuller Murrieta taste and it is consequently more expensive but a good Crianza 1978 from this vineyard is available from the Sherston Wine Company. Now this two-Marqués race has been joined by a third marquess, the Marqués de Cáceres, also in the Rioja Alta, whose whole range of wines, from Crianzas, Reservas and Gran Reservas, are now galloping ahead both in quality and popularity, although I personally find that his more expensive Reservas and Gran Reservas can be beaten by other vineyards. But his Crianza is superb – Laymont and Shaw has the 1976 imported by the Sherston Wine Company.

Perhaps I should explain a few technical terms. Rioja wines divide into Marca, which covers all the ordinary drinking wines entitled to the Rioja label, Crianza, or 'nursing' wine, which comprises the lighter drinking vintage wine, Reserva, which is older and heavier, and Gran Reserva which has been at least eight years in cask. But these descriptions give little guide to quality. It is possible to find horrible, muddy liquids tasting of vanilla essence and iron which are quite entitled to the Gran Reserva label, while the rarest and most sought-after wine in the whole of Spain, called Vega Sicilia, from its own wine region about twenty-five miles east of Valladolid, is entitled only to the humblest description of all, as Vino de Mesa. Spaniards have paid over £2,000 for a bottle of the 1920 vintage, and it is almost unprocurable here. I have never tasted it, and doubt whether it is worth the effort.

Apart from Vega Sicilia, the only Spanish wine worth getting excited about outside Rioja comes from the Penedès vineyards of the Torres family. Laymont and Shaw have a huge choice of them, from the delicate and grapey dry white Viña Sol 1981 to the huge, scented Gran Coronas Reserva Black Label.

Although Spanish wines never have quite the complexity of the best clarets, and some of their most expensive ones are marred by the horrible taste which they call 'oaky' and will remind any English drinker of vanilla essence and toffee apples, the truth remains that they are making some superb wines at every level, and beating the French by a huge margin all along the line. Here are my own favourites, all of which come from the Rioja Alta around Haro, where the best producer of all, in my experience, is the Compañia Vinicola de Norte de España, also called CVNE (pronounced Coonie).

For a light but elegant luncheon wine, I choose Viña Alberdi 1978, which is most cheaply available from Laymont and Shaw. This is my normal daily drinking wine. In winter, I prefer the fuller Muga Crianza 1976 from Sherston Wine Company. The best Burgundy-style Spanish wine I have yet discovered is CVNE's Viña Real Reserva. The best heavy claret taste I have found is called Reserva 904 1970 from La Rioja Alta – which is in fact a Gran Reserva. Prices for these wines vary, but it would be silly to pretend that part of the joy of Spanish wine is to think how much money you are saving.

Spanish Steps

I have decided to concentrate on Spain's second, much smaller wine region around Penedès in Catalonia, where wine-making has been revolutionised in the last twenty years – chiefly by the family Torres, singled out by Hugh Johnson in his *Pocket Wine Book* as the best of the Penedès wine-makers. But, whereas several of these wines are excellent, and spectacular value for money, one or two are utterly foul. If you buy blind and hit a bad one you might easily decide to make the simple equation in your mind, Penedès = piss. It is extraordinary how obstinate people are in their decisions. I know several sophisticated wine-drinkers who will absolutely refuse to consider whole new areas of wine production because the first bottle they tried was no good. But some of these Penedès wines, as I say, are really excellent, and they are on the whole cheaper than their equivalent quality from Rioja. All the wine-buyer needs is an independent guide who will taste them all and advise on which to try and which to avoid. That, as I see it, is the humble role of the wine correspondent, book reviewer or theatre critic in our society. Others may have a more exalted view of the critic's role – to *interpret* a wine, book or play, provide a political or socio-economic explanation for it all. But I feel our job is that of the taster at the medieval banquet. If we turn green and choke on our vomit, it is a sign that the revellers should skip that course. Here, at any rate, is a run-down on the full Torres range – obtainable (by the case) from Laymont and Shaw. Several of the wines are also available at Sainsbury's, Waitrose, Victoria Wines and Peter Dominic.

White

1 1984 Viña Sol (dry)
2 1983 San Valentin ('medium')
3 1983 Gran Viña Sol (dry)
4 1984 Viña Esmeralda (fruity)
5 1981 Gran Viña Sol 'Green Label' (dry)

Rosé

6 1983 De Casta Rosada (dry)

Red

7 1981 Tres Torres
8 1981 Coronas
9 1978 Gran Sangre de Toro
10 1979 Viña Magdala
11 1979 Gran Coronas
12 1977 Gran Coronas 'Black Label'

Report

Although there were two whites, Nos **1** and **4**, thought worth buying – with No **4** in particular being of exceptional interest – the reds came out best on the whole. Nos **7** and **12** are both recommended – **7** for everyday drinking, **12** as an impressive hefty wine – and **11** may comfort the nouveaux pauvres; but the prize goes to No **9**, the 1978 Gran Sangre de Toro, as a first-rate example.

Tasting Notes

1 Cheap whites are notoriously dangerous, but this one is clean, fresh and fruity, erring on the waterish side – which is much better than erring on the side of chemical and sugar additives. As the March Hare might remark, it is the *best* water. Comes with a black plastic bull.
2 Comes with a pink plastic Cupid. Utterly disgusting. Sugar and water, no fruit. Torres should be ashamed of himself. To be avoided at all costs.
3 Heavier than No **1**. Not quite as fresh. Slightly chaptalised taste. Less good.
4 This cross between two Alsatian grapes (Muscat and Gewürztraminer) gives a most unusual and rather delicious wine. Masses

of fruit – might be too sweet for some tastes – but excellent, well-chilled, as an aperitif. I did not find it too sweet to drink with a cheese soufflé; in fact it went very well. A jolly interesting, strong-tasting wine and a good idea to mix these two grapes. Highly recommended.

5 This is the sort of heavy oak-vanilla taste which the Spaniards think high-class, but I prefer my Horlicks without dust and cobwebs.

6 An acceptable but undistinguished rosé. Full, a bit sweet, better and cheaper than many Anjou rosés, but it soon cloys as an aperitif and I can't see any obvious reason for choosing it with food.

7 A good, lively red wine for slurping down at this price. Nothing nasty in it. Plenty of rivals available, from Italy, Provence and all over. Perhaps the plastic bull will help tip the balance in its favour.

8 Slightly sharper and higher-class. Good quality for price.

9 The most Spanish of the reds – hefty, dark and full of fruit as well as oak. Some might find it too heavy for its pretensions, but there are no tinny or coppery undertones and I found this a resplendently honest, clean, dark, strong wine – more honest and clean than many Châteauneufs-du-Pape (which it rather resembles), at half of the price of a known Châteauneuf and much better quality than many. Unqualified recommendation.

10 In their endless search for the right formula, the Torres have mixed the Pinot Noir grape from Burgundy with the Carignan grape from less favoured regions in Languedoc. I found the Viña Magdala, with its dreadfully cheap label, a little disappointing after the Gran Sangre de Toro. It is a perfectly respectable wine, which refugees from Burgundy might manage to take on board, but there is not much there to rave about.

11 55 per cent of this wine is Cabernet Sauvignon grape and it is a good, concentrated, high-class wine. It has no great acidity or *oomph!* but is a quietly comforting wine for those who like the rich taste without being able to afford it.

12 Torres has had a spectacular success with this flagship Reserva. Its 1970, entered for the Gault-Millau Wine Olympics of 1979 (with twenty-seven French judges and only two Spanish), came top of the top class in a field which included the 1970 Latour and 1961 La Mission Haut-Brion. It was at that point that Miguel Torres could claim to have changed the wine maps of Spain. Unfortunately, his claim is reflected in the price. This example has 90 per cent Cabernet Sauvignon, 10 per cent Cabernet Franc – the same cépage as can be found in many châteaux of the Médoc. Oddly enough, although obviously trying hard to be French, it ends up more Spanish than number 11, with a hefty, rather sweet, hot-country attack.

PORTUGAL

Any Port in a Storm

In an age of powerful wives and diffident husbands, it seemed that the English port-drinking habit might be going to go the way of so many London clubs, forced to close or merge through lack of attendance in the evening. For all the talk of collapsing marital observance, husbands are kept on a much tighter rein than they used to be. Wives had long regarded the English convention, whereby men stayed behind after dinner over their port, as some sort of anti-female conspiracy. First we were told it was unkind to the servants to sit too late. Then, when servants disappeared, we were told it was unkind to the women. Why should we wish to avoid them?

The few houses where the convention is still observed seldom provide the best male company, in any case, being composed either of unregenerate, red-faced and sometimes quite speechless pheasant-bashers, or nasty young merchant bankers who want to shout at each other about money. But I maintain it is quite a sensible practice, especially if the men do not stay behind more than twenty minutes, since it gives the company an opportunity to regroup and talk to other people than their next door neighbours at table.

Port, as foreigners are only just beginning to learn, is a most excellent after-dinner drink, although I have never found even the best tawnies (let alone the whites, which seem to me a complete waste of time) much use as an aperitif. It tends to cloy unless one has something to eat with it – preferably cheese or nuts. Another thing which is upsetting the port habit is the new, continental fashion for eating dessert after cheese. This has much to be said for it from the food angle, but it destroys the whole wine arrangement since most of the strong, fermented cheeses can be accompanied by

Any Port in a Storm

nothing but port; nobody wants to drink vintage port with strawberry tart; and nobody wants to go back to dessert wine after drinking port.

The only solution to this agonising problem is not to eat pudding. This often offends your hostess who has wept salt tears over her millefeuilles pastry all day, but there it is. Women who wish to please men (and there are still a few of these glorious creatures around) must simply learn how to do it. As the Age of the Bossy Wife gives way inexorably to the Age of the Single Woman, I observe that many single women now serve perfectly decent wine. But practically none serves port in any form, let alone decent port. Women still regard port as their natural enemy, even in an age which has acknowledged that it may be drunk in mixed company. I do not know of any single woman, even among the rich, semi-professional poules de luxe on the fringes of cafe society, who actually serves good vintage port. When, as Vanessa Redgrave used to sing, will they ever learn?

Having said which, I must agree that it is not without obvious dangers. Britain is the only country in the world where it is quite normal for many of the old professional and upper middle classes to start drinking at six in the evening and go on drinking non-stop until they go to bed at twelve or twelve thirty. The Japanese may drink into the small hours, but they start much later, and in America (where port scarcely features at all, let alone vintage port) only obvious alcoholics drink anything like as much as the ordinary English professional man. I honestly feel that after two glasses, even the best port begins to lose its edge. The endless circulating of decanters was always a great mistake. It made men stupid and noisy, it impaired their walking ability, their bridge, their sexual appetite, it often made them bad tempered and it always made them unpleasing to women. Even nowadays, there is always a temptation to drink a whole decanter when two old friends are together and the port is a particularly good one, opened in honour of the occasion – contrary to the general belief in Britain's hotels, vintage port does not improve in the decanter. In fact it starts dying within twenty-four hours of being decanted. After five days, the best vintage port in the world tastes little better than grocer's crusted, although wood ports seem to survive in bottle rather better – say two or three weeks after opening.

Now for the specifics. Those who cannot afford vintage port, or who cannot be bothered with all the business of storing and decanting it, should find a good tawny. Ruby is nothing but an inferior, younger form of tawny and generally comes under the heading of a low taste, although it is much favoured in certain quarters as a flavouring for surgical spirits, when it is called Red Biddy, and is said to drive you mad, then blind, before killing you. All the other ports, whether called vintage-character, or crusted, or late bottled, or special reserve, are inferior versions of the vintage port experience and proclaim your poverty to the world – which is not, really, the purpose of serving port.

A good tawny, on the other hand, is a magnificent drink in its own right, proclaiming the host's good taste and lack of ostentation. Two excellent tawnies are Cockburn's ten-year-old from most retailers, and their twenty-year-old tawny, Director's Reserve. The shippers of Cockburn's, Harvey's of Bristol, continue to produce my own two favourite tawnies – Harvey's Hunting Port in the cheaper range and their Director's Bin, which I honestly believe to be nearly as good as the forty-year-old Taylor's, which can sell at more than twice the price and is generally thought to be the best in the field.

Where vintage ports are concerned, it is absurd to buy the 'great' years (currently 1955, 1963 (just ready), 1970 (wait a few years) and 1977 (wait fifteen years)) when they are ready to drink. Prices, however, always start leapfrogging when these 'great' years approach maturity. For those without much storage space, the 1966s are drinking very well now, only slightly less good and less than half the price. Try a Quinta do Noval 1966 from the Wine Society. Next to come up will be the 1975s – drinking long before the 1970s. Berry Bros offer Cockburn, Croft, Dow, Fonseca, Graham, Quinta do Noval and Warre, to name but a few.

The smartest thing for those with storage space (and spare cash, patience and life expectancy) to do about vintage port is to buy enormous quantities of their favourite port, preferably from the shipper, as soon as a 'great' year has been established. There are often false alarms, as all declared vintages are liable to be hailed as 'great' at first, even the extraordinarily light 1975s, but it is now obvious that the 1977s are going to be genuinely great, like the 1963s and possibly the 1970s. Most shippers still have stocks of the

1977. Through my own wine broker, the diligent Colin Price-Beech, I was able to secure a load of Warre's 1977. The great thing about vintage port is that some fools always drink it too young. I feel reasonably confident that in ten years' time I will be able to sell half the load at four times the price paid, invest the difference in whatever is the new 'great' year and in due course, on this system, be able to drink the very best vintage port free for the rest of my life.

For those without storage space or free cash, the best way to enjoy the vintage port experience is to concentrate on the single quinta wines produced by the great houses in 'off' years. The two best, in my experience, are Taylor's Quinta de Vargellas (shipped by Deinhard) and Fonseca Guimaraens (shipped by Mentzendorff). The Vargellas 1972 is around nearly everywhere – Grants of St James, Lay and Wheeler of Colchester, Berry Bros, Key Markets. The superb 1969 needs hunting for. Bibendum offers the Fonseca Guimaraens 1968, and it is sometimes possible to find the 1964 around, which I found marvellous. The point about these wines is that they really are just as good as any but the best vintage wines ten years older, and you can bet your life that nobody, or practically nobody, will know the difference.

Hard to Port

Cockburn's launched their 1983 vintage port with an incredibly grand tasting of every Cockburn vintage declared this century – fifteen of them in all – while throwing in the 1863 vintage for good measure. Two things struck me as I tasted my way through: first, there was not a dud wine among them – not even the 1975 which people have tended to sneer about; secondly, that in an uncertain world, vintage port is one of the very few things which never deteriorates, increases in value and can always be guaranteed to give an extremely agreeable experience at the end of the day. If the purpose of money is to provide joy, it is hard to see why anyone spends money on anything else, except to relieve the consequences of over-indulgence. It occurred to me that with the parlous state of Britain's economy in the long term – I honestly believe that when North Sea oil dries up in fifteen years' time, we will none of us be able to buy any of the classic wines of France ever again – heavy investment in vintage port now might provide the best guarantee of a tolerable middle age. I made the same calculation about 1982 clarets and 1983 Burgundies, but they will be over long before the 1977 vintage port, for instance, reaches its prime, and one has one's late middle age to consider, as well as the butterfly years in between.

Money invested in fixed-interest securities might just as well be handed over as a present to the politicians, while equity shares leave you at the mercy of an increasingly idle, disaffected and greedy workforce. Works of art have to be insured and are at any event liable to capital gains tax, not to mention the hideous profits of auctioneers, dealers and the whole rotten structure of the art world with its poseurs, perverts and squabbling crooks. Wine folk, by contrast, are delightful, honest, kindly, clean-living people of natural enjoyments, as I was able to confirm recently on a visit to Taylor's Vargellas lodge in the upper Douro valley, where all the best wine is made which goes into the most highly regarded of all the vintage ports.

Taylor's vintage port is also the most expensive, but there is much to be said, where wine investment is concerned, in going for the most expensive. I notice that Berry Bros and Rudd are now selling Taylor's 1977 for £22 the bottle, against £13 for a 1977 Gould, Campbell, for instance. This price of £22 represents an increase of 100 per cent on what you would have paid if you had ordered the wine F.O.B. from Deinhard, the shippers, 29 Addington Street, SE1 (261 1111), when it was declared in 1979. In other words, if you had bought it then you could now sell off half your stock and reckon to drink the other half for nothing in twelve or fifteen years' time, at whatever grotesquely exalted price it will command then.

Cockburn did not declare a 1977 vintage so one cannot compare price movements, but it is also a first-class port, like Fonseca, which is galloping up on the inside track price-wise. Cockburn is shipped and sold by Harvey's of Bristol. Fonseca 1983 is shipped by Mentzendorff, but can be ordered through Market Vintners.

Punters can make up their own minds, but I suspect it may be necessary to move fast. The last vintage declared by Taylor and Fonseca – Cockburn did not declare it – was 1980, which strikes me as much thinner and less appealing. I honestly believe that the 1983 may prove to be the last first-class vintage which many people in England will be able to afford – even without the ever-present danger of a socialist government which will reduce the pound to ten cents while slapping import controls on anything worth buying. The main port houses are already beginning to talk about allocations for the 1983, and I suspect that its price will have doubled within a year of its being landed.

To explain why I am so gloomy about the future of vintage port – quite apart from the dangers of our own economic collapse – I shall have to return to my visit to Vargellas, in the upper Douro. Vargellas, as I say, although a smallish quinta of 100 planted hectares, is generally reckoned as the jewel in Taylor's crown, producing the best wine of the most highly priced vintage in the world. In off-years, Taylor's sometimes declare a single-Quinta da

Vargellas vintage and this represents one of the best bargains in all the vintage ports. Berry Bros stock the 1967 and the 1965 – both superb – while it might still be possible to find an odd bottle of the 1972 around Key Market or Gough Bros stores.

Vargellas, producing the best port of all, is obviously an extreme case, but the demand for Taylor's vintage has never been higher and, mutatis mutandis, its problems are the same as those of all other vintage port growers. Its vines are planted in extraordinarily inhospitable soil, haunted by phylloxera; every vine must be grafted on another, whose roots sometimes go ten feet or more under the earth before finding sustenance. The vineyards are steep and inaccessible and although they are among the most beautiful I have ever seen, they would be unworkable in any other country. Portugal has the lowest wages in Europe, even including socialist Yugoslavia, less than half the gross national product per head of Ireland. The cultivation of these vines and making of the wines – grapes are still trod by foot, on the grounds that any other process breaks the pips – are not only absurdly labour intensive but also require a degree of industry and fortitude which is unthinkable in any advanced Western country – unless, like oil-riggers, the workers are paid £400 a week.

Portugal has now joined the Common Market. This can only mean more industry, higher wages, and the slow death of the port business as we know it – what premium is left will probably go into the process known as late bottled vintage which, although a pleasant enough drink, has nothing whatever to do with vintage port in its final presentation. At one tasting I even mistook a late bottled vintage for a standard ruby and I was not drunk at the time. Although much fuller than the standard ruby, it has the same pasteurised smell, being frozen at one point in manufacture.

Perhaps late bottled vintage is really all we deserve. It has the advantage for publicans and hoteliers (not to mention moderate port drinkers) that, being more or less inert, it does not alter much after being opened and can hang around in the bottle for several weeks. As I say, it is a pleasant enough drink, although I much prefer a good tawny.

Both Cockburn and Taylor market a dry white port, but I prefer the sweeter whites myself. Taylor has been pushing out its 'Chip Dry' white port for fifty years now, always hoping it would catch on, but it never has, and I doubt if it ever will, although it is a well-made wine and makes a good aperitif with tonic water and a slice of lemon. Perhaps we should call it Fizz and Chips.

But nothing will ever beat the splendour of a grand old vintage port. The Vargellas 1965 is as good as anything we are likely to see in our own homes. I shall be eternally grateful to Mr and Mrs Alistair Robertson of Taylor's for one important discovery. I always thought that more than two glasses of vintage port made one bad-tempered. In their company I discovered that if everybody is drinking it, and the mood is right, one can happily put away eight or nine glasses.

Not Port

Portugal's reputation as a serious wine-maker has been all but ruined by the filthy gas-pumped, sugared-up, Mateus Rosé from SOGRAPE at Vila Real, but one occasionally hears grudging praise for their prickly, fresh Vinho Verde made from barely ripe grapes. It drinks better in Portugal than over here, and then only if the maker has refrained from adding too much sugar. The Bucellas Velho 1979, from the Caves Velhas just north of Lisbon, is an altogether more serious wine. It has a good, strong, elegant, hot-country taste without any touch of sharpness and dies on the taste of water, rather than cloying or hanging around. It was noisily appreciated by my panel who voted 7:2 in favour of it as a wine on its own merits, 9:0 in favour of it as value for money.

The Dão Reserva 1974 has an excellent nose with a good, dark colour and lives up to it with a smooth finish. It was elected unanimously and there is really nothing to be said against it except that at this price it is obviously lighter than the Romeria Garrafeira 1974. A 'garrafeira', Hugh Johnson tells me, is the 'private reserve' aged wine of a merchant, usually his best, often produced by mixing. I certainly would not have guessed that was its meaning. Anyway Mr Romeira has produced an altogether richer and grander smell for his garrafeira. The taste is fuller and more generous too, although I did not feel it had quite delivered all its promise. Of the two, I think I would go for the lighter Dão as being the more successful in its admittedly slightly humbler class. Perhaps it is just snobbery which made me wonder if the garrafeira was quite rich enough or grand enough for its pretensions. My neighbour referred to it mysteriously as a 'bit of a cockteaser' but she may have been suffering from an incipient migraine. It is certainly a good, concentrated and rich wine.

THE REST OF THE WORLD

Strine Wine

Australian local patriotisms are hard to cater for if one has never visited the place. The more I learn about Australian wine the more impressed I am by it, particularly since the devaluation of the Australian dollar by a factor of nearly 50 per cent has made them so attractive to thirsty Englishmen. Even so, they are not to be found in the cheapest range of wines, which will rule them out for about 80 per cent of wine-buyers, but in the range of £4 to £8 or £10 a bottle I would say they offer the best value for money of any major wine region in the world.

However, in waxing more and more lyrical about Australian wines, I have tended to treat their outlandish names, which to the Australian ear no doubt have the music of the great communes of Bordeaux and Burgundy, as if they all came from one and the same place, that is to say, Australia: Barossa, Keppoch and Coonawarra; Tahbilk, Geelong and Bendigo; Rutherglen, Riverina and Mudgee.

Then I received a slightly hurt telephone call from a Senator Mrs Amanda Vanstone, of South Australia. Was it a coincidence, she asked incredulously, that in all my writings about Australian wine, I had never mentioned her own state, which contained the biggest wine-producing area in the whole continent? Her voice suggested I might have been taking bribes from the neighbouring states of Victoria and New South Wales to ignore hers, but before I could assure her that I hadn't, she said she was delivering a case of South Australian wines for me to taste.

For those who, like me, have never been to Australia, I can reveal that the first three names in my glittering roll-call above – Barossa, Keppoch and Coonawarra – belong to South Australia; the second three belong to Victoria; the third belong to New South Wales.

Strine Wine

One problem with Australian wines is to persuade English drinkers to take them seriously. For a romantic dinner party for two, with the music playing softly and the lamps turned down, a bottle of Brown Brothers' Koombahla Cabernet or Penfolds' Coonawarra or Smith's Yalumba 1978 might be just the thing. They are all excellent wines, but your guest could just as well decide you are pulling his or her leg, that your intentions are not romantic at all. For these tender moments I always recommend a conventional bottle of good expensive white Burgundy. It is just possible but pretty hard to find a bad Meursault or Puligny-Montrachet of 1982 or 1983. White wine is every bit as intoxicating as red, but less obviously so; everybody knows that Meursault and Puligny are good and expensive (with white Chassagne-Montrachet you have to be more careful) and there is an aura of Quiet Good Taste surrounding expensive white Burgundy which will never attach to Smith's Yalumba Chardonnay, however hard they try.

But it would be wrong to suppose that Australian wines lack chic among English folk who take their wines seriously. Australia's equivalent of Château Latour is Penfold's Grange Hermitage, described by Hugh Johnson as 'The one true first-growth of the Southern Hemisphere.' Although made from Shiraz (i.e. Syrah) grapes, it tastes much more like the familiar Cabernet/Merlot/Malbec mix of Bordeaux.

What is reputed to be the best of the Australian Chardonnays, also from the state of South Australia, is made at the Petaluma winery in the foothills of Adelaide. Examples of its famous 1983 vintage are available from Les Amis du Vin and La Vigneronne. Perhaps I should warn that these Australian wines are absolutely delicious when young – say after two or three years – but they do not have the staying power of a white Burgundy. Possibly because they lack acid, they die very quickly. I tasted a wonderful 1980 Brown Brothers' Chardonnay (from Milawa, in the neighbouring state of Victoria) at Cullen's, which seemed, in 1983, to beat anything I had tasted from the Beaune region for a very long time. It had all the fruit and spice of a Montrachet or a Corton-Charlemagne with the undertones of butter, flint and cigar smoke which one finds in the best Californian Chardonnays. In great excitement, I bought a couple of cases and began to notice after six months how they seemed to be tasting slightly less delicious than I remembered. I still have a few bottles left and they are dead as mutton, tasting of stale cardboard.

But the same is certainly not true of South Australian reds, which should be kept for as long as possible. The trouble is that they are fruity enough to drink when very young, so that few people ever get to learn what they are capable of becoming. The oldest you are likely to find in the shops is a 1976, but 1978s and 1979s are still quite common. Petaluma produces a Cabernet/ Malbec blend which is said to be excellent, but I have never tasted it. The best I know, also from South Australia, is Stanley Leasingham's 1979 Cabernet/Malbec called Bin 56 from Avery's. Yalumba's Signature Reserve Cabernet Shiraz 1978, from the Wine Studio, is another memorable South Australian experience.

The cheapest drinkable Cabernet Sauvignon from South Australia I have been able to trace is called Hardy's Captain's Selection 1983 from Majestic Warehouses. This is a fuller, better wine than you can normally find at the price; the vulgarity of the label would probably give it a certain added chic in young circles.

My advice is generally to leave the Rhine Riéslings alone, although the Australians are immensely proud of them. It seems to me the Germans do them better and cheaper.

My final conclusion, having spent a month on wines from the state of South Australia, is that they are no different from the wines of Victoria, New South Wales and Western Australia. At any rate, I could identify no distinguishing characteristics; high, cool vineyards generally produce subtler, cleaner wines but there are examples of these high vineyards in all the states. The standard of wines, however, is extremely high, and the value for money impressive. One might feel foolish laying down a wine called Smith's Yalumba 1978 for another five or six years, but I feel it would be a sensible thing to do. However, until I visit the country I shall continue to refer to Australian wines as if they all come from the same place.

Good News from Lebanon

The good news is that the next two vintages of Serge Hochar's Château Musar – 1979 and 1980 – have arrived from the Lebanon. Many will already know of my passion for this strange, rich wine from Lebanon which I swear tastes like something between a hot-season Latour, a grand and ancient Hermitage and one of those magnificent old 'cooked' Burgundies bottled in England which have now all but disappeared from the market. Served at the right temperature (if, like me, you live in an icebox they should be several degrees above room temperature) and decanted at least two hours before drinking, they are my idea of a taste of heaven. They also keep forever, and are the cheapest and best way of ensuring that we have plenty of good wine to drink in the years ahead when, after the exhaustion of North Sea oil, we suddenly realise that we in Britain will never again be able to buy serious wine from anywhere.

To put these two new arrivals in perspective, my panel tasted them against the Musar 1977 and 1978. Of the four, the 1978 seems the one with least future. Nothing will be lost by drinking it now. The 1979 is richer, deeper and fuller, perfectly good for drinking now although I suspect it will go on improving for many years, as the 1977 has been doing in my cellar. While the 1978 is now showing all its charm, I feel it will grow firmer if kept, and might easily overtake the 1977, which is already quite unmistakably a great wine.

The 1980 is in a different dimension. It is less overwhelmingly rich than the 1979, but more elegant with a multiplicity of tastes such as one expects only from the very best Bordeaux. One would be making a grave mistake if one drank it for another year or eighteen months. Neither the tannin nor the acid has yet found its proper level, but the fruit is pure Cabernet Sauvignon with all the wonderful complications which that grape can offer. Those who sneer at the tastes of Cinsault and Syrah in the classic Musar will find it absent from this 1980, which has less of a Latour about it than the promised subtlety of a Lafite. I do not blush to bandy these names around when discussing a wine which may yet prove to be M. Hochar's finest, if least characteristic, achievement. Other Musars are easy to spot at a blind tasting because of what my daughter has called the Red Cross lorry element, but the 1980, when at its peak in about five years' time, may well fool them all. The 1979, as I say, is already delicious to drink, but the 1980 is still comparatively hard going.

Some Californians

I had thought to polish off Californian and Spanish reds in a single section with a little faint praise and some sneering remarks about the poor. No doubt they would taste quite nice but so does ginger beer. Who could be expected to pay attention to bottles with names like Firestone, Inglenook, Stony Hill or Z-D Wines, let alone hold a serious conversation with them? Anybody who has been to California will know that it is simply not on. An incomprehensible stream of egomaniac psychobabble, punctuated by long silences, is not what is meant by conversation, at any rate in Europe. It was inconceivable that a wine from California would have anything to say to a cultivated European gentleman beyond some straightforward advice about vaginal hygiene, sanitised lavatory seats and the rest of it.

Instead, I find myself facing a personal crisis with roots in the cultural identity of us all. There can be no doubt that the Californians, for all their psychobabble and personal hygiene, are producing very good red wines indeed. They may not yet be within striking distance of the very, very best, for reasons which I shall try to explain, but pound for pound they offer better wine cheaper than most of the Upper Second châteaux of Bordeaux characterised in Hugh Johnson's indispensable *Pocket Wine Book* by three stars. Nothing I have yet tasted deserves a fourth star, although Johnson awards a couple.

The first bottle to arrive came from the exporter, Glovers of San Francisco, who had sponsored a huge Californian banquet at the Dorchester which I was unfortunately unable to attend, being in the Far East (even the Japanese are making quite reasonable wine nowadays). It was called Stag's Leap No. 2 Cabernet Sauvignon 1978 from the Napa Valley. I ask you. Call it Boar's Rush, Bull's

Californian Wines

Pounce, Sheep's Droppings No. 1 from the Nappy Valley... But I had to admit it tasted very nice. Quite exceptionally so, in fact.

Then Messrs Corney and Barrow sent me a second bottle of the same stuff, with another from the same vineyard (Stag's Leap Merlot 1978) and I realised we were in the middle of a major cultural crisis. The wine is quite simply better than its equivalent from Bordeaux – say a Château Cos d'Estournel 1970 or, in the case of the Merlot, let us say a Château Canon, St Emilion 1970.

Yet can one honestly serve Stag's Leap to one's friends? Few, if any, have much sense of taste. They would assume one was skimping; if they discovered how much it had cost, one would be the laughing stock of the *vieillesse dorée*. Of course it would be the easiest thing in the world to pour the stuff into a Cos d'Estournel or Château Canon bottle, but where is the fun of that? It is the sort of behaviour which sets its perpetrator off on a very slippery slope and can bring about the end of a civilised society as we know it.

It is not just snobbery, or the joy of rolling familiar French names around in our throats, which makes us instinctively prefer the proper stuff. There is also a subtle failure in the Californian wine to achieve either the grandeur or the rudeness of its French equivalent. A serious bottle of claret will assault you with half a dozen impressions, some pleasant, others less so: after black-currant, you may suddenly be rocked by a heavy mouthful of earth, a smell of pepper, or a distinct taste of rotting beechwood. This is probably because of filthy French habits – not washing their hands before wine-making, working with a dirty, yellow cigarette hanging out of their mouths, breathing garlic over the wine press, etc. Even the best Californian wine has only one taste – delicious but homogenised, clean but somehow unexciting. One really can't be more poetic about them than that. I am afraid it may be the result of too much hygiene.

But does one really want these ancient, inalienable tastes of rats' mess, toadstools and pickled frog skin to survive? That is something we must all decide for ourselves. The French themselves are in two minds. Looking up the Stag's Leap wine cellars in the wine drinker's bible, which is Serena Sutcliffe's edition of André Simon's *Wines of the World*, I see that the Stag's Leap proprietor, Monsieur Warren Winiarski, walked away with all the prizes at the 1976 Paris tastings, causing consternation among the Bordeaux growers. That was for his 1973 vintage. The 1978 is considerably better.

Enough of this. The plain truth is that if you are after a nice taste in the mouth, rather than some maundering nostalgia trip, California generally offers better value for money than Bordeaux. The best and commonest grapes are Cabernet Sauvignon and Zinfandel – their Burgundy-style, called Pinot Noir, is still a bit irony and crude, but getting better all the time.

And from Chile . . .

People keep telling me that good wine is made in Chile, but I have never found one before. The Viña Linderos is made from 100 per cent ungrafted pre-phylloxera Cabernet Sauvignon 25 miles south of Santiago, and advertises itself rather engagingly as being 'without oak wood taste'. I think 'oak wood taste' may mean something different in Spanish, where it is applied to the unpleasing toffee-apple and vanilla effect on some Gran Reservas. This wine has a beautiful, dark red colour and dry depth of Bordeaux flavour. I would not be ashamed to serve it (suitably decanted) at a dinner party for anyone except a serious wine expert I was trying to impress. There is really no need to tell anyone it comes from the Southern Hemisphere, or to invite people to try drinking it when standing on their heads. It is exactly the sort of wine which should make people thank God for South America.

PEOPLE AND PLACES

The Cellars at Annabel's

The cellars of Annabel's Club are not to be found, as one would suppose, underneath the beautiful building in Berkeley Square, where the thump of dancing feet might disturb the repose of those stacks and stacks of venerable bottles: 12,360 bottles of claret; 2,628 bottles of red Burgundy; 7,392 bottles of white Burgundy; 2,064 bottles of champagne; 1,428 bottles of miscellaneous wines – as well as a Private Room, which I was not invited to visit, where 6,000 bottles of unknown wine are mysteriously stored.

Behind Berkeley Square there runs Hays Mews, full of dinky little Georgian cottages where once the coachmen and chauffeurs lived. Now it is mostly offices, with a few private houses for the very rich and very discreet. Somewhere in that mews is another door which might lead anywhere, but in fact leads straight into a lift shaft which drops without warning thirty or forty feet under the surface of Mayfair. The lift is an ancient iron contraption which moves with agonising slowness and the sort of groans and howls you would expect to hear if it was being pushed by a score of Christian slaves under the lash of a Mohammedan buccaneer. It is the only means of entering or leaving the Aladdin's cave which stretches away in galleries like a Roman catacomb as far as the eye can see. Instead of ancient Roman bones, they contain racks and racks of bottles ... Château Latour from sixteen vintages between 1911 and 1976, Cheval Blanc from thirteen vintages between 1934 and 1970, including in both cases the brilliant 1947 and 1953, and the 1961 which is now so highly priced that most people can only dream about it. I recognised with a pang the Cheval Blanc 1966 which, although less famous than the 1961 and the 1970 (which I have not yet tasted) happens to be the wine which persuaded me, some years ago, to devote the rest of my life to wine.

The Cellars at Annabel's

Mark Birley accompanied me to the cellars – in his elegant London suiting and immaculate tie from ... Charvet? Hermes? Turnbull and Asser?, he reminded me somewhat of a Victorian father making a rare visit to the nursery where a child is dying of scarlet fever. His purpose was to introduce me to Mr Brian Davies, the cellerman for the past twenty-three years. He must have been there when the 1961 Bordeaux were being wheeled in: Latour, Cheval Blanc, Léoville–Las Cases, Pichon Baron and Phelan Segur are the ones that survive. I wondered what wines he had seen wheeled out. The Latour can be bought at Annabel's for £400 the bottle; the Cheval Blanc at Mark's Club for £300; the Pichon Baron at Mark's Club for £140, the Leoville–Las Cases at Annabel's for the same price. Annabel's seems to be doing rather better there. The Phelan Segur is not offered at either – no doubt being held back for a year or two, as all these wines should be, really.

The rarest and the best of all were not in evidence – no doubt they are hidden away under some weighted flagstone, possibly with a poisoned blade on a spring catch to protect them against thieves. Somewhere in that mysterious catacomb, as I learned from a computer print-out of the stocks, were some bottles of the great 1945 vintage in Bordeaux: Petrus, Mouton-Rothschild, Margaux and Cos d'Estournel. Many serious wine-drinkers would give their eyes – or at any rate a little finger – for any of these. The interesting thing about 1945 is that it is the last year, by my reckoning, that the prodigious price rises for famous wines of famous years actually represent an increase in quality. Any table wine which survives after forty years is something of a freak: it cannot be expected to improve. And 1945 – like 1961 – was quite simply as good a year as the world has ever known. On the same day that I visited the cellars in Hays Mews the first of a series of international wine auctions was planned at the Cafe Royal, where one bottle of Lafite-Rothschild 1911 was expected to fetch anything between £17,000 and £22,000. For a serious wine-drinker, such prices are simply a joke. But the same auction had a single bottle of Petrus 1945 expected to fetch between £800 and £900. And *that* represents some serious wine-drinker's expectation of a good drink.

'I don't think you want to talk too much about the *value* of the wine', said Mark Birley who, like most Londoners, lives in terror of burglary. I should have thought he was safe. No burglar in his senses would risk that murderous lift, which announces anyone's presence much more thoroughly than the geese of the Capitol. It would take them ages to find the valuable wines which lie among 37,000 assorted bottles, and they would have to know their vintages pretty well to sort them out. Somehow I do not see a British burglar sitting with Hugh Johnson's *Pocket Wine Book* or Oz Clarke's *Webster's Wine Price Guide* sorting through 37,000 bottles to separate the corn from the chaff, and then sending it up in that groaning, howling lift to a pantechnicon parked in Hays Mews.

The cellar master, when I met him, was not at all the sort of figure I had expected to meet in this strange catacomb stretching underneath Mayfair. I had half hoped for a boss-eyed hunchback clad in russet with huge keys clanking at his waist. Although Mr Brian Davies has been living in these cellars for twenty-three years he is a spry, cheerful man, unbowed by the grandeur of the wines gently maturing around him. My first question to him was rather out of the side of my mouth, as I was accompanied by my namesake and distant kinsman, Mr Harry Waugh, the immensely distinguished doyen of the English wine trade who still supervises wine purchases for Annabel's, Mark's Club, the Ritz and one or two other favoured establishments. I had been inspecting the Annabel's wine list and thought it rather short on good Burgundy. My cousin is famous as one of the greatest living experts on Bordeaux, and I did not want him to hear his pipsqueak kinsman querying his judgement on Burgundy.

Mr Davies's answer was brief and to the point: 'When you're talking about a night club, you're not talking about red Burgundies', he said. 'White Burgundy and Bordeaux are easily the best sellers. Always have been.'

Even so, although there are one or two excellent 1971s, most of the red Burgundies on the lists of both Annabel's and Mark's Club are wines from slightly off years. Compared to the excellence of the Bordeaux selection, these seemed to me rather sad. I am a Burgundian myself, and I was alarmed to see an extensive listing of wines from the Domaine de la Romanée-Conti – the most expensive of all Burgundies – from the disastrous year of 1975. These wines are a notorious trap for the unwary. The Domaine had no business to declare a vintage that year. Practically no other respectable wine-maker in Burgundy did so. It should have sold off its horrid, rot-filled liquid as Côte de Nuits or even Bourgogne Rouge and recouped on the excellent 1976 vintage. Anybody who knows anything about Burgundy avoids these wines like the plague. Yet here they are, appearing on the otherwise resplendent wine lists of Annabel's and Mark's Club: Annabel's offers the Echézeaux, the Grands Echézeaux and the Richebourg 1975; Mark's Club offers the Echézeaux; kept in reserve is a La Tâche 1975 which I must admit I have never tasted. From its reputation, I would judge that the kindest thing to do with this filthy wine, after ten years, would be to pour it down the sink.

The white Burgundies, I should explain, are quite excellent, including some inexpensive examples, like the Mâcon Lugny 'Les Genièvres' from Louis Latour of both 1981 and 1983, which would be a tremendous boost to wine-lovers at a night club. The range of choice among white Burgundies is quite enormous, with none of the over-priced rubbish which it is easy to find in this over-subscribed corner of the market. What surprised me is that although the list offers a house Chablis and a house St Emilion (from Moueix, quite easily the best wine-maker in St Emilion and Pomerol) it offers no house champagne.

In my experience, on the whole, one drinks champagne at night clubs. At an expensive and smart night club like Annabel's, one would expect champagne to be the main tipple for those who are sitting around the dance floor, rather than having dinner. Obviously one expects a selection of the expensive 'prestige' champagnes – Dom Pérignon, Roederer's Cristal, Perrier-Jouët's Belle Epoque and Krug Vintage (I was sorry to miss my own favourites, Bollinger RD 1975, Laurent-Perrier's Grand Siècle and Krug Grande Cuvée) – but most punters will tend towards the cheaper end of the market, and there the list has nothing but well advertised marques whose price is necessarily reflected in the promotion behind them. In fact there are dozens – perhaps scores – of smaller champagne houses making really excellent champagne who do not spend a farthing on promotion and whose prices are consequently about three-fifths those of the famous brands. Some are noticeably better than, for instance, the Taittinger Brut, Charles Heidsieck or Canard-Duchêne non-vintages which comprise Annabel's bottom offer. But there is not only more profit to be made from selling a low-priced champagne – a de Telmont, for instance, or an Alines Grietien, even a Billecart-Salmon or an Henriot – with a new Annabel's Special Cuvée label, there is also more pleasure for the punters. These lesser-known wines are actually better, and at the lower price they should encourage more and more people to drink champagne, which is surely a good thing. Spirits make them morose, and even the best still wines, drunk into the small hours, make their breath smell.

Apart from these two weak areas – in red Burgundy and good house champagne – the range of wines on offer is quite stupefying. Walking away from that extraordinary catacomb in Hays Mews, I found myself wondering how it came into existence, with its only entrance a James Bond-style lift-shaft which screams like a soul in torment. Its ends are now sealed off, but I would like to think they used to connect with the cellars of Beconfield House, at the very end of Hays Mews in Curzon Street. This building is now the chief headquarters and barracks of MI5, the home security and counter-espionage service. I would like to think these cellars were the dungeons and torture chambers of that strange organisation where I believe the late Ian Fleming spent many happy hours during the war torturing captured German naval officers. Or so my father used to tell me. Perhaps he got it wrong. It adds a certain je-ne-sais-quoi to the thought of people ordering these fabulously expensive wines in Annabel's brought up on the groaning lift, if the walls which had been storing them all these years had also witnessed scenes of abominable cruelty committed by our fellow-countrymen. Our island story rolls on. Times change, and we all change with them – a little bit, in any case.

Luxury London and its Wine Merchants

Those with houses in both England and France will know that they drink better French wine in England. There are two reasons for this. One is that the exorbitant English duty on wine, which is the same for a bottle of plonk selling at £2.20 as it is for a bottle of decent Burgundy selling at £8.00, means that the difference in price between good and bad wine is much smaller. In France, the same bottle of plonk will cost 45p, the same bottle of Burgundy about £7.50. The other reason is that the French, being greedier and more impatient, tend to drink their wine too young.

As a result, London is the more or less undisputed centre of the world market in fine old French wines. New York is catching up, especially since the strong dollar made Americans so rich, but New Yorkers seem exclusively interested in the great 'prestige' labels – the five Bordeaux premiers crus, which are Châteaux Latour, Lafite, Mouton-Rothschild, Margaux and Haut-Brion, two grands crus of St Emilion and Pomerol – Cheval Blanc and Petrus – and of course the ludicrously over-priced Château d'Yquem in Sauternes. Among Burgundies, American buyers seem interested only in those grands crus which have the magic words 'Romanée-Conti' somewhere on the label – La Tâche, Grands Echézeaux, Echézeaux, Richebourg, Romanée-St Vivant, Le Montrachet (white). The result is that those wines listed above are now grotesquely more expensive than any others, and English buyers are mad to touch them.

So far as Americans have any genuine preferences in taste, it would appear to be for the Pomerols. Château Petrus has now overtaken even the five premiers crus of Médoc in price, with the result that it can scarcely be bought in London at all. The London agent for Petrus, Messrs Corney and Barrow, refuse to quote a price on any of their twelve vintages in stock, saying only that prices are available on application. I would advise English buyers at the luxury end of the market to leave it well alone – at any rate, to the Americans and Arabs – and try Corney and Barrow's excellent Châteaux Trotanoy instead, at about quarter the price.

In Burgundy, the same considerations apply, that anybody seeking after the best in London should avoid anything from the Domaine de la Romanée-Conti, because the Americans have already tripled its price. Magnificent grand cru Burgundy of 1976, 1972, 1971, 1970 and even 1969 for those who insist on the best, can be bought from most of the wine merchants listed below. Names to look for are Corton Bonnes Mares, Musigny, Chambertin, Vougeot, Clos St Denis, de la Roche or de Tart.

The odd thing about champagne, often thought of as the most luxurious of wines, is that although it is hard to find a drinkable example for less than £9–£10, the very best champagne seldom costs more than two and a half times as much. This ratio of about 2:5 to 1 between the very best and the cheapest could not be more different from the situation in Bordeaux, where it works out at more than 70 to 1. Under the circumstances, I am surprised that more people do not serve good champagne, thinking they can save money on any old filth. Many people trying to cut a dash with champagne serve the 'prestige' or 'luxury' labels – Moët's Dom Perignon, Roederer's Cristal, Taittinger's Comtes de Champagne. The first two are specially popular with showbiz folk. I have nothing against the wines, but feel the bottles are rather vulgar. A vintage Krug, or Veuve Clicquot-Ponsardin, is the best one can or should do.

Of the wine merchants, Berry Brothers at 3 St James's Street, SW1 is generally agreed to be the grandest among ordinary snobs, if not among wine snobs. If you go to Buckingham Palace you will more often than not be given a wine from Berry Brothers, although it is only one of many royal warrant-holders in the business, including Justerini and Brooks, Saccone and Speed, Corney and Barrow, of London, Harvey's of Bristol, etc. In fact, Berry Brothers are probably the cheapest of the high-class wine merchants in London, with a particular line in minor clarets and excellent Beaujolais which they bottle themselves. They are pleasant and efficient to deal with, and still give credit.

Justerini and Brooks, also of St James's Street, is used by the sort of male person who has his hair cut at Truefitt and Hill, Saccone and Speed by ex-Guards officers, but I have never been able to think of any good reason for patronising them. The best for German, Alsatian and Rhône wines in London is Loeb and Company, of Jermyn Street. The genuinely grandest wine merchant for the wine snob is probably Corney and Barrow, with every wine traced to its grower and vineyard in a catalogue which reads like some French medieval Book of Hours. But I confess I find their prices a trifle disconcerting.

Pretty grand people buy their wine at auction – Christie's and Sotheby's both hold regular sales – which is nearly always much cheaper for old vintages, while the very grandest people have an agent to buy it for them in France, straight from the grower, and then put it down for ten or twenty years in their own cellars. Other luxury lovers shop around among the sort of clubs and emporia I have mentioned – Wine Society, Les Amis du Vin, Malmaison – looking for bargains. They are still to be found, although for those who really know their wines, some of the best bargains – and some really excellent wines – are in the multiple chain stores like Victoria Wine and Peter Dominic. Unfortunately these people are not really geared for the luxury service.

Celebrating with the Wine Trade

Wine merchants, whatever their other failings, are generally quite a festive crowd. We may feel, as we pay their shocking prices, that some element of celebration is required with every bottle drunk, but they seem to live in a perpetual state of celebration through selling it. In 1985 they were delirious with excitement over a stupendous 1983 vintage in the Rhône, which they say is as good as the 1978; even if the best reds from Hermitage and Châteauneuf-du-Pape should not be drunk for the next fifteen years, the wine trade is getting ready for it with a series of Rhône celebrations.

One of the best ways to drink expensive wine, in my experience, is at these celebrations. Some of the best are held at L'Escargot restaurant at 48 Greek Street, W1, and whole weekends devoted to wine are held at the Castle Hotel, Taunton.

Both were celebrating the Rhône in 1985. At L'Escargot, Steven Spurrier kicked off with a champagne-style, rather heavy effort from the north Rhône called Saint Péray. My own feeling about non-champagne sparklers is that they are none of them quite good enough to drink undoctored (i.e. with brandy, sugar and angostura or peach juice or orange juice or Kir) and this Saint Péray, which is almost unprocurable in Britain anyway, would be too expensive to doctor. Hugh Johnson, who looked in at the party, recommended a Crémant de Bourgogne as the best of these sparklers, and I traced an example to Corney and Barrow.

After the St Péray at the Escargot thrash we drank a 1982 Condrieu from the small firm of E. Guigal to go with raw ham and figs. Condrieu is one of the least well known and most delicious wines of France, but it is not cheap. Les Amis du Vin have one from the firm of Georges Vernay, and Robin Yapp had another in 1982 from the great Viognier. I earnestly recommend all serious drinkers of white wine who have not discovered Condrieu to give it a whirl before the Americans discover it. Still in the north of the Rhône, we drank a 1978 Hermitage, also from Guigal, with grouse. This is the sort of wine which blows your head off and should be kept for at least ten years. The 1978s are getting expensive and hard to find, but it is a magnificent wine, still underpriced for the quality.

Next we went to the Southern Rhône for a beautiful example of Jaboulet's Châteauneuf-du-Pape Les Cèdres 1966. This is one of the wonders of southern France – a rich, full, slightly burned taste experience which makes one really happy to be a wine-drinker. I still possess a bottle or two of the even better 1967.

We drank the Châteauneuf with a toasted goat cheese in salad, and then moved to a pineapple business with cinnamon bananas with which we drank a Muscat de Beaumes de Venise – a flowery, very alcoholic sweet drink – which has become all the craze recently, even reaching Sainsbury's. I still think the best example is Vidal-Fleury's which is available all over the place but which I first discovered at the Hungerford Wine Company. Corney and Barrow offer a very superior one indeed from Leon Chival which has a smell like some millionaire's orchid house. The cognoscenti, I am told, are moving on to a Muscat from Portugal called Moscatel de Setúbal which is cheaper and less alcoholic, but although I have seen it in one or two catalogues I have not yet tasted it.

The joy of these wine dinners is that one has splendid food and the company of other wine maniacs, who tend to be a most agreeable collection of people.

Celebrating with the Wine Trade

The Académie du Vin Wine Course

Steven Spurrier is one of those enterprising young Englishmen who, in earlier times, might have spread terror among the fat galleons of the Spanish main as a privateer. Finding opportunities restricted in this particular field, after Rugby and the LSE he set up as a wine merchant in Paris, founding the highly regarded Caves de la Madeleine where he sells the French their own wine as cheekily as any burglar claiming his reward from an insurance company. After a few years of this, he decided that the French did not know enough about their wine and set up his own Académie du Vin in Paris to teach them.

His course was designed not only to impart everything they should know about the buying, storing and serving of wine, but most important of all, how to appreciate it. The French flocked to his door, and now he has started similar courses at the Académie du Vin in New York and at the Christie's Wine Course in London.

However, although a few besotted amateurs may be prepared to pay the price of these courses, they are really for professionals: people in the trade, *sommeliers* and would-be wine-writers. Now Mr Spurrier, in association with his partner, M. Michel Dovaz, has produced the whole operation in a book, so that anyone who wishes to become a wine expert can study at home on a do-it-yourself basis.

The *Académie du Vin Wine Course*, published by Century in association with Christie's Wine Publications, starts with a Foundation Course, teaching us how to taste wine and giving the basic information about making it. Next the intermediate course introduces us to the various grape varieties (becoming more and more important to the wine-drinkers as New World wine-makers increasingly label their products by the grapes used – Cabernet Sauvignon, Merlot, Syrah, Chardonnay, Chenin Blanc, Muscadet, Sémillon, Riesling, Gewürztraminer, etc.) and a tour of the world's major wine-producing areas. Next the Advanced Course takes us once again through all the major grape varieties, tasting half a dozen examples of each, from the classic wines of France to the newest arrivals from Australia, Italy and California. It also takes us through most of the types of wine, and on some highly serious 'vertical' and 'horizontal' tastings of red Burgundy and claret. In fact the book supplies everything needed to become a wine expert except the wine.

Mr Spurrier remedies this defect at a great annual banquet in Paris, for which tickets may be bought (write to him at 25 rue Royale, Cité Berryer, 75008 Paris). The problem with being a do-it-yourself wine expert is that wine can only be bought in bottles (or sometimes half-bottles) and to buy a bottle each of all the wines offered at these jamborees would probably cost at least £400, even before one started thinking about the food. The Académie du Vin's dinner this year was held at the Pré Catalan, a very swish two-star restaurant in Paris's Bois de Boulogne, and included a tasting of 1982 clarets beforehand.

The meal itself, when it arrived, was a real feast, such as would be impossible to find under other circumstances. After a fancy petite marque champagne, we drank a Château Laville–Haut-Brion, Graves 1966 with a feuilleté d'écrevisses. This is a curious wine, disgusting when young, made from 60 per cent Sémillon (the grape used for all the great sweet white wines from Sauternes) and 40 per cent Sauvignon, the general workhorse Bordeaux dry white grape.

Next we had two 1970s, the Haut-Bailly (Graves) and the Léoville-Barton (Saint Julien) with a foie gras frais en feuille de choux. Mr Anthony Barton, the Irish owner of Léoville-Barton, was sitting at my table, so one did not like to say that his 1970 was still a little closed up and hard (although not nearly so tight as the Haut-Bailly) but the foie gras en choux was a revelation. I had supposed, on reading the menu, that feuille de choux referred to some pastry preparation, but it actually meant a cabbage leaf. Who would have thought to put fresh foie gras – surely the most delicate taste the French have developed – in a cabbage leaf? Only, apparently, Monsieur Patrick Le Notre, of the Pré Catalan.

Next, with a magret de canard – an over-rated example of nouvelle cuisine, I maintain, which contrives to make duck taste like beef entrecôte – we drank a 1970 Gazin from Pomerol and a 1971 Château Figeac from St Emilion, both of which were superb. Neither, however, could hold up a candle to the 1962 Léoville–Las Cases which arrived with the cheese. The meal was finished off by a pretty, very nouvelle cuisine-ish plate of red fruits accompanied by a 1975 Château d'Yquem. This was the first time I had tasted the 1975 d'Yquem, and traditional wisdom in England would maintain that this was far too young to drink such a great Sauternes. By coincidence, however, I had to be in London at lunch next day with Messrs Corney and Barrow, the City wine merchants, who very kindly produced a 1947 Yquem with an excellent, neutral dessert of mangoes. Most people agree that 1947 was an even greater year in Sauternes than 1975. My conclusion was that although both were unforgettable, the English gain nothing by keeping their Sauternes for years and years before drinking it. Age may lend the madeirised, slightly burned flavour of an expensive Trockenbeerenauslese, but nobody can seriously suppose that the Riesling grape has anything to teach the Sémillon, and age certainly detracts from the stunning fruitiness of the younger wine.

All of which may seem a somewhat grand and irrelevant conclusion to draw, since few people now will be in a position to try a 1947 Château d'Yquem, and even the 1975s are pricing themselves beyond the serious wine-drinker's range. But it might influence our attitude towards the 1972 Sauternes, still buyable and said to be even better than the 1975s.

An Aside

According to Michael Broadbent, who is a Master of Wine and supervises Christie's Wine Department, the best wine really only begins to develop – open out, show a leg or whatever – once it is in the glass. Within a space of two hours a wine which has lain undisturbed for twenty or thirty years will run the gamut through tight, suspicious puberty, vivacious adolescence, joyful awakening, sensuous maturity, fat and crumbling middle age to sour, crabbed old age.

Of course he is absolutely right but I had never thought of it before. I always imagined it was some failure in *me*, or the result of what I had eaten, which made the best wine turn to gall after two hours and created the world-hunger for vintage port.

At any rate, I pass on this important piece of wisdom from one of wine's grand old men. I met him at the climax of a Wine Weekend at the Castle Hotel, Taunton, where a magnificent dinner was accompanied by what is called a 'horizontal tasting'. This does not mean that you taste it in the Geoffrey Wheatcroft position, but that you take five or so great wines of the same year and try making bogus remarks about them to show you can tell the difference. On this occasion we took the five premiers crus of Bordeaux for 1953 – Haut-Brion, Latour, Mouton-Rothschild, Margaux and Lafite.

Mr Broadbent pronounced Lafite the winner. 'I have followed this wine since she was a lovely baby, a lively toddler, a graceful teenager, and now she is a lovely, *beautiful* woman', he said tearfully. For those who want to give the lady a whirl, I must sadly report that the wines are almost unprocurable elsewhere, although I see that Reid Wines, of Marsh Lane, Hallatrow, Bristol, who specialise in golden oldies, offer the sainted Lafite.

Evelyn Waugh's Wine

For a man whose life revolved around wine, Evelyn Waugh wrote surprisingly little on the subject. Even his novels have surprisingly few references to his lifelong passion, although there is a famous passage from *Brideshead Revisited*, when Charles Ryder, staying with his friend Sebastian, 'first made a serious acquaintance with wine and sowed the seed of that rich harvest which was to be my stay in many barren years'. Many will remember the scene when they sit up late in the Painted Parlour, getting their glasses more and more muddled as their praise for the wine grows wilder and more exotic:

'. . . It is a little shy wine like a gazelle.'
'Like a leprechaun.'
'Dappled, in a tapestry meadow.'
'Like a flute by still water.'
'. . . And this is a wise old wine.'
'A prophet in a cave.'
'. . . And this is a necklace of pearls on a white neck.'
'Like a swan.'
'Like the last unicorn . . .'
'Ought we to be drunk *every* night?' Sebastian asked one morning.
'Yes, I think so.'
'I think so too.'

Goodness knows how many sottish late-night conversations that passage has inspired among later generations of Oxford undergraduates, but I feel it belongs among the immortal pieces of wine-writing, along with Thurber's famous caption, from *Men, Women and Dogs:* 'It's a Naive Domestic Burgundy, Without Any Breeding, But I Think You'll be Amused by its Presumption.'

One might also deduce from the scarcity of Evelyn Waugh's writing about wine that it belonged to that part of his life which he regarded as private. The fierceness with which he defended his own privacy gave rise to many of the stories – gossip columns were full of them – which portrayed him as a monstrous old blimp, roaring and yelling at any intruder into his private domain. In fact he was a gentle, humorous man – sometimes sad, sometimes gloomy – and nowhere near as bad-tempered as he appeared to the Press and public on his few excursions outside the small world of family and friends. But I do not think it is betraying a trust to reveal an aspect of his private life which will be of great interest to wine-drinkers and which has never, so far as I know, been revealed before.

The mid-life crisis is familiar among males in our society. Many mark it by leaving their wives of many years and taking up with some luscious young dolly bird or, if they are not married (like Bernard Levin) they may give up their work and go to live at an *ashram* in Poona. Evelyn Waugh celebrated his own mid-life crisis first of all by going mad soon after his fiftieth birthday, in January 1954. This episode is well documented in his novel, *The Ordeal of Gilbert Pinfold*, first published in 1957 but available in Penguin. Next, having recovered his sanity, he sold his house and moved to the huge icebox at Combe Florey, in Somerset, where I now live. In the process, he suffered a violent change in his wine-drinking habits which was to remain with him for the rest of his life – he died in 1966 – as the only permanent trauma from his experiences at this time. From that moment, he could never touch a drop of claret, under any circumstances.

It would be interesting to know if others have had the same experience in middle age. His house in Gloucestershire was famous for the excellence of its clarets – as for its vintage ports – but just before moving house, in the late autumn of 1956, he sold every bottle of claret in his cellar, and never bought another. Worse than this, he could not bring himself to drink any red wine from Bordeaux even in the house of friends. Some time ago I found myself sitting next to Sir Hugh Greene, the former Director General of the BBC. Like the Ancient Mariner, he held me with his skinny hand and told me a tale of woe which had understandably been haunting him for years. It appeared that at some time in the early 1960s, probably 1963, Evelyn Waugh had visited the BBC to make a broadcast about P. G. Wodehouse, and Greene had decided to give a dinner party at Broadcasting House. In Waugh's honour, Greene had procured rather a special bottle of claret – not just rather a special bottle, but the classic, never-to-be-forgotten Cheval Blanc 1947 – with the possible exception of Petrus 1961, surely about the most Burgundian bottle of claret which Bordeaux has ever produced. Evelyn Waugh thanked him very much, but declined to take any. End of story.

Plainly, this violent repudiation of the world's second best wine-producing area was the result of some psychological trauma, if not actual brain damage. He was quite happy to experiment with wines from unlikely places like Chile (probably of Cabernet base, although in those days they did not specify the grape) and once discovered a new enthusiasm for the red wines of Germany. Even more shaming than that, he came back from Rhodesia one day announcing a new discovery from Portugal called Mateus Rosé, and drank it through one whole summer. Whenever challenged with this, I loyally maintain that the Mateus Rosé of the late 1950s was a quite different wine from the sugary pink fizz of today, but I do not honestly know where the truth lies.

At any rate, no claret ever entered the cellar at Combe Florey until 1971, when I moved back. At Evelyn Waugh's death in 1966 he left four or five dozen Chambertin 1955 from Berry Bros – a magnificent wine, but one which would have improved with keeping in less frigid surroundings than the cellars at Combe Florey. Although, so far as I know, no wine has ever actually frozen solid down there, I cannot think why not as the temperature in his day was frequently below freezing point. He also had two cases of Richebourg from the same source – I think the vintage was also 1955 – some odd parcels of rather old Sauternes, notably Suduiraut 1947, a lot of champagne, notably Clicquot Rosé for which he had developed an old man's passion. There were no bottles of vintage port and nothing else.

I think I may have one clue, which is neither psychological nor biochemical, for Evelyn Waugh's repudiation of claret. For some reason, he always referred to it as 'clart', even in such homely expressions as 'to tap the claret', meaning to draw blood in a fight. 'Have a glass of clart', he would say. Some had difficulty in understanding what he meant, but he persisted. Then in 1956 there was published a rather shameful book called *Noblesse Oblige*, edited by Nancy Mitford, with contributions from herself, Waugh, John Betjeman, Christopher Sykes and others, discussing the characteristics of the English upper class. In the course of his contribution, Sykes – who was a friend of my father's, despite being, as he frequently pointed out, of better breeding – mentioned 'a Gloucestershire landowner' who believed 'that persons of family always refer to the wines of Bordeaux as "clart", to rhyme with cart'. Mr Sykes opined that 'this delusion' showed 'an impulse towards gentility' which might be preferable to the contrary impulse, among true aristocrats, towards affecting the mannerisms of the proletariat.

My father spotted the reference to himself immediately, and although he took it in good part, it must have left him in something of a quandary. Either he had to drop his harmless affectation in deference to the mockery of a younger man and lesser artist, which he did not deign to do, or he had to persist in the awareness that everyone was sniggering at him as the Gloucestershire landowner who said 'clart' when he meant 'claret'. I do not know how much influence it had on his subsequent behaviour, but it is fact that within a year he had sold not only his house in Gloucestershire but also all his claret, and never touched the stuff again.

I cannot leave the subject without touching on Evelyn Waugh's wine-writing, such as it was. His main contribution to the field (I exclude his work on a history of Veuve Clicquot) was a booklet called *Wine in Peace and War* published by Saccone and Speed in 1947. It has never been reprinted, and has little of contemporary relevance in it. I observe from his correspondence with his agent, A. D. Peters, that he was paid at the rate of twelve bottles of champagne per 1,000 words – not an immensely generous rate, I would say. Perhaps that explains why he wrote so little on the subject. I am sure he could have done better.

The last thing he wrote about wine appeared in the New York *Vogue* in the year before he died. It dealt with champagne, and described the circumstances in which it should be drunk: 'For two intimates, lovers or comrades, to spend a quiet evening with a magnum, drinking no aperitif before, nothing but a glass of cognac after – that is the ideal ... The worst time is that dictated by convention, in a crowd, in the early afternoon, at a wedding reception.'

That comment strikes me as profoundly true. Immense harm is done to champagne by the English habit of drinking it, usually warm and in a sort of trifle dish, at weddings in the early afternoon. That is why so many people in England claim to dislike champagne.

An even profounder claim is made in the first writing I have been able to trace by Evelyn in the December issue of 1937, under the title 'Laying Down a Wine Cellar':

Wine lives and dies; it has not only its hot youth, strong maturity and weary dotage, but also its seasonal changes, its mysterious, almost mystical, link with its parent vine, so that when the sap is running in the wood on the middle slopes of the Côte d'Or, in a thousand cellars a thousand miles away the wine in its bottle quickens and responds.

I wonder if there is any truth in this theory. We have all noticed extraordinary variations from bottle to bottle within a matter of a month or two, but I have never thought of relating them to seasonal changes in Burgundy, Bordeaux, the Lebanon or wherever. Perhaps it is true that many wines – not ports nor old-fashioned 'cooked' Burgundies – go to sleep in the winter. If this is true, we should drink Australian, South African and Chilean wine throughout the winter, French wine only in the spring and summer months. Californian wines, by the same token, can be drunk all the year round.

Or perhaps it is all a load of codswallop. I was never entirely convinced that my father, for all his poetic gifts, knew very much about wine. Certainly his brother, Alec, knew much more. When Evelyn wrote those words, he was just laying down his first cellar. My grandfather, Arthur Waugh, who was a publisher and critic, drank nothing but Keystone Australian Burgundy, a beverage which he believed to have tonic properties, much to the embarrassment of his two sons.

Even so, my father, who wrote in 1937 that 'nothing is easier than to ruin a fine wine by careless handling', was among the worst offenders in this respect. He never brought up a wine to the dining room more than half an hour before a meal – not that it would have made much difference if he had, as the dining room was nearly as cold as the cellar; and he never opened a bottle before it was time to drink it. In his last years he drank splendid Burgundy, day after day, at temperatures which many would judge too cold for Sauternes.

But the saddest part of the article, written as a young man of thirty-three, concerns ports of a great vintage: 'it is at least fifteen years before they become drinkable, and fifty before they are at their prime; some superlative vintages will live a century. It is these vintages which one should buy as soon as they are shipped and lay securely down for one's old age, or for posterity.'

Perhaps he had rather lost his enthusiasm for posterity by the time he died, at the sadly young age of sixty-two. Despite his golden opportunity to lay down the 1963 vintage before his death in 1966, he left no port at all.

WINE MERCHANTS

Adnams
The Crown, High St., Southwold, Suffolk IP18 6DP
Tel: (0502) 724222

Les Amis du Vin
7 Ariel Way, Wood Lane, London W12 7SN
Tel: 01 743 2066

Avery's of Bristol
7 Park St., Bristol, Avon BS1 5NG
Tel: (0272) 214141

Berry Bros & Rudd
3 St James's St., London SW1A 1EG
Tel: 01 930 1888

Bibendum
113 Regent's Park Rd., London NW1 8UR
Tel: 01 586 9761

Corney & Barrow
12 Helmut Row, London EC1V 3QJ
Tel: 01 251 4051

Cullen's
142 Battersea Park Rd., London SW11 4NB
Tel: 01 622 4467

Grape Ideas
3–5 Hythe Bridge St., Oxon. OX1 2EW
Tel: (0865) 722137

House of Hallgarten
Carkers Lane, Highgate Rd., London NW5 1RR
Tel: 01 267 2041

Hedges & Butler
153 Regent St., London W1R 8HQ
Tel: 01 734 4444

Hungerford Wine Company
128 High St., Hungerford, Berks. RG17 0DL
Tel: (0488) 83238

Laymont and Shaw
The Old Chapel, Millpool, Truro, Cornwall TR1 1EX
Tel: (0872) 70545

Market Traders
11/12 West Smithfield, London EC1
Tel: 01 248 8382

O. W. Loeb & Co.
64 Southwark Bridge Rd., London SE1 0AS
Tel: 01 734 5878

Le Nez Rouge Wine Club
12 Brewery Rd., London N7 9NH
Tel: 01 609 4711

Recount Wines (Colin Price-Beech)
44 Lower Sloane St., London SW1
Tel: 01 730 6377

Reid Wines
The Mill, Marsh Lane, Hallatrow, Bristol, Avon BS18 5EB
Tel: (0761) 52645

Sherston Wine Company
1 Church St., Sherston, Malmesbury, Wilts. SB16 0LA
Tel: (0666) 840644

La Vigneronne
105 Old Brompton Rd., London SW7 3LE
Tel: 01 589 6113

Windrush Wines
The Barracks, Cecily Hill, Cirencester, Glouc. GL7 2EF
Tel: (0285) 67121

Wineheads
18 Kenway Rd., London SW5
Tel: 01 244 9900

The Wine Society
Gunnels Wood Rd., Stevenage, Herts. SG1 2BG
Tel: (0438) 314161

The Wine Studio
9 Eccleston St., London SW1W 9LX
Tel: 01 730 7596

Yapp Brothers
The Old Brewery, Mere, Wilts. BA12 6DY
Tel: (0747) 860423

INDEX